CONQUERING M.

HOW TO SOLO TRAVEL THE

WORLD FEARLESSLY

BY

KRISTIN ADDIS

ISBN: 9781651056912

Design by Kristin Addis and Ashley Yap

First Edition: June 2016

Second Edition: December 2018

2 3 4 5 6 7 8 9 10

TABLE OF CONTENTS

INTRODUCTION

*White sand beaches. Drinks with paper umbrellas.
Mountains, deserts, and forests. Exotic cities with even
more exotic food. All tempt you day in and day out in your
Instagram feed and Facebook updates, and on your
Pinterest boards. Nary a moment passes where the world
doesn't beckon you to explore it.*

So what's stopping you?

Maybe it's time. Maybe it's money. Maybe you've asked
your significant other, best friend, sister, brother, former
roommate, second cousin once removed, that girl you
kind-of-sort-of know from first period senior year... and
they all told you they couldn't go with you.

*You're left with two choices: wait — potentially forever —
for a travel buddy to join you, or cast out on your own,
armed with nothing but what you can carry and your own
wit.*

Both scenarios sound scary.

I found myself in the same situation in 2012, waking up at
odd hours to Google far-off places and daydreaming of
Asia instead of focusing on spreadsheets at work. I was
obsessed with the idea of traveling the world.

As a young girl, I read historical novels about foreign
places, like *The Poisonwood Bible* and *Memoirs of a
Geisha*, played video games like *Civilization* and *The*

Amazon Trail, and even searched out weather forecasts across the world just to get a sense of what it might feel like to live there.

My family didn't have the resources to travel internationally during my formative years. We often vacationed in Yosemite, just a day's drive from where I grew up in the suburbs of Los Angeles. We sometimes visited family in Hawaii when there was a deal or funds were available. But that was rare.

It wasn't until I turned 20 and visited Europe with my sister that I got my first taste of international travel.

It was as wonderful as I had always imagined it would be.

Exploring the Mezquita in Córdoba — whose architecture I'd just studied in college — and beholding the green, rolling hills in Galway that I'd only seen in movies cemented a love that I'd always suspected was inside of me: a love for exploring the world outside.

With my sister and our friend Angela in Córdoba, summer 2006

One year later I graduated from school and moved to Taiwan to study Mandarin. Eight months after that I came back home to get a "real job" as an investment banker, because that's what I thought adults were supposed to do. I stayed for four years, working at a job I never loved.

I injured my shoulder at the gym in my fourth year at the firm, when I was 25. My doctor told me that I'd need surgery, and that the recovery would take a full year. That meant a year of barely any of the exercise I'd come to enjoy — no diving, no hiking with a backpack, no Pilates, and no yoga. It was possible I'd never be the same again. It was the wake-up call that made me realize that life is short and my health is not guaranteed. The recovery was long, and while spending nearly all of my time for several months in a reclining chair, I started to contemplate why a young woman should spend her youth in a cubicle — more or less the same restrained situation.

Chances are that you're reading these very words right now because you haven't given up on this dream of traveling.

During this time, I discovered and pored over travel blogs, and I realized that there were people just like me who were out there traveling — without trust funds, and even by themselves. After months of going back and forth mentally, losing sleep over the decision, and finally feeling it so strongly in my core that I couldn't think of anything else, I stared at the flight search results for the hundredth time and finally clicked, "purchase." I walked away from my job, boyfriend, and apartment with a one-way ticket to Bangkok and nothing but a carry-on backpack. It was terrifying.

Yet it all worked out, and five years later, I'm still traveling solo.

So you may be wondering: Should someone who has a perfectly steady job, one that others would be glad to have, walk away from the path to financial success? Should a woman in a stable relationship that could result in marriage walk away from a sure thing? Is it responsible to put savings into traveling rather than investing in property with a white picket fence and a porch swing for two?

Chances are, though, that you're reading these very words right now because you haven't given up on this dream of traveling. You're questioning whether there are options out there other than the typical path, and you're looking for guidance on how to make your travel dreams a reality.

When I began the process of putting this guide together, I asked myself what exactly I would have wanted to read before taking off of my solo journey. What I would have needed the most was reassurance that I would be OK saying goodbye to everything I had ever known and striking off on my own. At each step, I would have wanted the guidance of experienced travelers who had been in my shoes. I would have wanted someone to tell me exactly what to do.

The result is this guide. It took months of researching and years of first-hand experience traveling to come up with the information, tips, and tricks outlined in this book, thanks to my own experience and that of other women who contributed.

In this book, I break down the monumental task of such a big lifestyle change into manageable pieces. We'll explore all of the ways to prepare for a solo journey so that you can be not only prepared but confident, excited, and exhilarated for the road ahead. We'll discuss getting over the fear, confidently sharing the news of your decision to travel, tips for preparing financially, what to pack, how to stay safe, and how to avoid loneliness, among other topics.

This is the beginning of a wild, beautiful, and fulfilling ride, fellow traveler!

— Kristin Addis

From Armchair to Airline Chair: Taking the First Steps

"The most difficult thing is the decision to act. The rest is merely tenacity. The fears are paper tigers. You can do anything you decide to do. You can act to change and control your life and the procedure. The process is its own reward."

—AMELIA EARHART, the first female aviator to fly solo across the Atlantic Ocean

Getting Over Your Fears

Perhaps the most difficult thing about preparing for a solo journey is the paralyzing fear of the unknown.

Several years ago, before I considered traveling solo, I had a conversation with a friend who had visited Hawaii alone.

"You went to Hawaii by yourself?!" I asked him. "Why would you want to vacation, especially in a tropical and romantic place, alone?"

He answered that he had gone because at the time, nobody else could join him; moreover, he wanted to be alone. Back then, I felt sorry for him, and even a bit scared, at the thought that anyone would have to go anywhere by him or herself.

I never imagined that I'd be doing the very same thing —
and enjoying it immensely — a couple years later.

Being alone is not something that I find easy. I tend to get
my energy from being around other people, and I always
feared that the road would be a lonely place. Nor is
making decisions about what to eat or where to go my
forte.

So how on earth have I managed to travel on my own? It
turned out to be a lot less daunting and lonely than I
thought. I just had to get over the initial fear first, and the
rest I learned on the go.

Fear accompanies just about every great life change.
Remember your first day of high school? I do: I was
terrified of going to a new school, where I'd barely know
any of the other kids. I agonized over what to wear,
worried I'd make a bad impression on the cool clique, and
I stressed over whether I'd like my new teachers or not.
The same thing happened on my first day of work. Was a
hair out of place? Would someone use a finance term I
had no familiarity with? Would everyone find out that I was
just a young girl with no real idea what she was doing?

Deciding to travel was much of the same: I worried I'd
make wrong turns, have bad days, and get lonely. In truth,
all of those things happened. But I was much more
equipped to deal with them than I realized. People are, in
reality, often much more adaptable than they believe
themselves capable of being.

Emily Moyer of the blog *Let's Roam Wild* says of her decision to quit and travel solo,

I was terrified. Scared I was making the wrong decision by giving up a promotion at my prestigious job, worried about what was going to happen with my relationship, unsure, honestly, of what my future would hold if I did decide to quit my job and travel alone. [But after traveling] I can now honestly say that if I die tomorrow, I lived my life exactly the way I wanted to. How many people can say that?

A healthy amount of fear is what pushes people to act in the first place. Perhaps it's fear of complacency, of living a life you didn't dream of, of missing out on adventures and sights that, if you wait, you may never get to have or see.

How do you conquer the fear mountain?

Find role models

The first helpful step to start getting over the fear is reading the accounts of others who are out in the world doing the very same thing that you want to do. Perhaps, like I did, you need to see that other women are successfully traversing the world on their own, safely and enjoyably. It can help to ease the worried mind to feel more understood, supported, and like you're not the only one with this crazy dream of traveling the world alone.

At the time that I was considering this life change, a friend of mine suggested that I read the blog *Bacon Is Magic* by Ayngelina Brogan, in order to become more confident and to have a female solo-traveling role model. She left a stable career in marketing and a comfortable life with her boyfriend to travel by herself through South America for a year. Her bravery was encouraging. While so many women in her position would feel pressure to marry that boyfriend, keep that job, and fill a traditional role at age 30, she decided to push boundaries and follow her dream instead.

Throughout her trip she remained open about the difficulties and the beautiful moments It was an honest account of a relatable woman who took a year for herself to explore both the world outside and the world within. She has since returned to her home in Toronto and once again has a career in marketing, along with a smattering of other roles, such as part-time restaurateur.

I wrote to her to ask about bravery and she said,

Readers thought I was extraordinarily brave, full of courage they didn't have. The truth is that when I started my trip I was afraid too — afraid I'd never find love again... afraid I was ruining my career. I was petrified, but I was more terrified of a life full of regret. It changed who I was as a person, and now I don't fear anything. And as for love, I met the love of my life on the road.

Role models in life are often what inspire people to move in the direction they want. To see someone successfully doing what you aim to do is a great way to allay fears and to gain some of the inspiration you need. Luckily these days there are hundreds of travel blogs, if not thousands, many of which are written by nomadic women who travel the world alone. Pick one — or a few — and get inspired.

Here are a few well-written examples:

- Be My Travel Muse by me!

- Adventurous Kate by Kate McCulley

- Alex in Wanderland by Alexandra Baackes

- Ashley Abroad by Ashley Fleckenstein

- Anna Everywhere by Anna Karsten

- Bacon Is Magic by Ayngelina Brogan

- Camels and Chocolate by Kristin Luna

- A Dangerous Business by Amanda Williams

- Girl vs Globe by Sabina Trojanova

- Helen in Wanderlust by Helen Davies

- Hippie in Heels by Rachel Jones

- Heart My Backpack by Silvia Lawrence

- Just Travelous by Yvonne Zagermann

- Legal Nomads by Jodi Ettenberg

- Paper Planes by Alana Morgan

- This American Girl by Camille Willemain

- This Battered Suitcase by Brenna Holeman

- Young Adventuress by Liz Carlson

Before I started traveling, I emailed a few solo female travel bloggers, looking for encouragement, and I was met with uplifting emails and a "safe place" for my feelings and fears. Don't be afraid to contact female solo travelers you don't know personally if you need encouragement. That's why the blogs exist, and sometimes the words of a perfect stranger will be exactly what you need.

If you're looking for advice, leave a comment on a blog post if you notice that the blog author tends to respond personally. Are you on Twitter? That's a great place to start a conversation with a blogger whom you admire. You can break the ice by simply asking a direct question about one of her tweets. Or if you feel scared and need support, send an email and be vulnerable, even if it feels a little strange to do so.

Personally, I was pretty raw and honest in my emails to bloggers while I was searching for support. I'll never forget the words of encouragement I received from Ayngelina of *Bacon Is Magic* and how much they helped me. She knew that I needed someone to tell me that it was OK to just go, so she did just that.

I receive similarly vulnerable emails all the time from readers, and I do my best to answer everyone. You might be surprised by how accommodating and comforting it is to reach out to women who are already doing what you want to be doing. And if you don't hear back, don't despair or take it personally, just reach out to someone else who inspires you. Eventually, someone will be happy to connect.

Trust yourself

My biggest fear before leaving was that I would be left high and dry if things went wrong.

What helped me to feel confident in my decision was remembering that at every step of my life up to that point, I had made it through. I had never had a failure so big that I couldn't overcome it. In fact, even the things that seemed like doors slammed in my face at the time made sense later. Everything had contributed to my growth somehow.

I thought back to articles that I'd read on the Internet about the regrets of the dying and realized that for most of them, their biggest regret was not honoring their deepest desires. Instead they chose to remain behind their desks. I didn't want to have those regrets too. I didn't want to wonder "what if?." That helped propel me forward.

I had survived all of the stumbling blocks previously, hadn't I? I had survived what felt like debilitating breakups, a shoulder surgery, and college classes that I thought would eat me alive at the time, and even in the darkest hours, I emerged again. In remembering all of the things I had accomplished, I had more confidence in myself to keep going.

I bet if you look back on your life, you'll notice the same pattern of overcoming obstacles.

Fortune favors the brave, after all. Empower yourself to be brave. Trust yourself!

Know that you're not alone

Even if it seems like nobody around you has been bitten by the travel bug, you can find your tribe, both at home and on the road.

In most major cities, particularly in the US and Europe, you can attend Travel Massive events that are attended by travel lovers, industry folk, and travel writers as well. The events are free and often take place at a local bar or incorporate a fun activity like biking or walking around the city.

You can also look at your local Couchsurfing events or even host a couchsurfer if you have the space. It's a great way to meet an international crowd without leaving your hometown. You can get travel tips and feel understood and like part of the traveling community before your trip even begins. Seeing so many people out living your dream will help you to remember that you're not the first to do this, and you're never alone.

I also find that highly interactive Facebook groups can feel like a fun and supportive way to connect with other women who love to travel. My current favorite is Girls LOVE Travel, where women share their photos, articles they love, videos they are inspired by, and questions they have about various travel topics.

You're not alone in your desire to travel, and the more you surround yourself with people who support your dream, the more it can take shape as reality.

Stay excited

Think about all of the goals that you have worked towards in the past. It felt darn good to finally reach them after months of toil, didn't it?

Whether it's weight training and focusing on a diet with more veggies and less sugar to get healthier, studying for weeks on end for a final exam that you end up acing, or finally getting the choreography right for a dance you've been practicing for months, it feels really good to reach a goal!

Finally going on your dream trip is no different, and at times when it feels hopeless or difficult, keep focusing on the prize and it will come more easily.

Imagine how good it is going to feel when you're finally seeing the Eiffel Tower with your own eyes, on that African safari, or hiking over that glacier in Patagonia. These are the experiences that you'll never forget, and you deserve it! When you focus on that, the things you have to overcome to get there will feel more like steps on a ladder than stumbling blocks.

As the 13th-century poet Rumi famously said, "What you seek is seeking you."

"What About My Career?"

"I don't get it," my best friend's boyfriend, Brody, said to her when she told him about my plans to quit my job and travel alone, "Why would Kristin leave behind a perfectly good job, a cushy life, and a beachside apartment that most people would kill for? Why would anyone want to walk away from that?"

I knew that at least one person, or even a few people, would have that reaction when I finally did share the news to my friends and family that I had plans to travel the world by myself. I was afraid that someone would try to talk me out of it, and I wanted to be as sure and steadfast as possible. I mentally prepared for the inevitable negative pushback for months leading up to the big reveal.

In reality the majority of my friends and family were very supportive of my desire to quit my job and travel. I was lucky.

However, Brody's words echoed my own thoughts: How can the break in the résumé be explained away? Will it negatively impact my job prospects when I come home if I leave and travel now? If I quit my job, will I be able to find one that's just as good when I come back? What will I do with all my stuff?

Selling everything off, quitting one's job, and riding off into the sunset in a blaze of glory sound all romantic and movie-like in theory, but the reality is that most people will return home at some point and will want to be able to get a good job when they do.

Jodi Ettenberg, former corporate lawyer turned Food Traveler's Handbook author, food tour leader, travel blogger, and T-shirt designer at the Legal Nomads blog, says,

The fear of trading a stable life and paycheck for uncertainty is a real and valid fear to have. It will be deepened by the many people who will likely tell you that you're crazy for doing so. That fear isn't something anyone can face but you. It's not easy, but if an unconventional life is what you want, there are ways to mitigate this:

- **Make plans for worst-case scenarios,** *and then get an elevator pitch in mind for people who doubt your choice. In my case it was that I had a law degree and could use it if needed; for others it's that they're graphic designers and can work from anywhere. For some it's a teaching degree. Whatever it is, it's good to rehearse how to handle negativity that comes your way.*

- **Work on the skills that make you desirable in your field.** *If you want to be able to leverage them to build the life you want, you have to be good at what you do. While I wasn't sure what I would do with my life after I quit my job, I did feel calmed by the knowledge that I had a skill set I could put to use in different professions.*

Developing the skills that make you a valuable asset professionally, both prior to and during your trip, can help to make your résumé stronger rather than weaker as a result of traveling.

While traveling I continued to develop skills in writing, photography, and marketing, taking unpaid writing opportunities at first in order to get my name out there. On long bus journeys and layovers, I read books about online media and learned about an industry I'd never had exposure to before. Like Jodi, I prepared myself for a return to full-time work.

I have been on the road for over five years now and have watched as hundreds of people I've met have returned home to stable careers and/or started entirely new businesses with ideas they developed while on the road.

Some even started businesses and maintained them while continuing to travel. My friend Dorian started an import business when he found decorative, handmade leather belts in India. Now each summer, during most major festivals in the United States, he makes several thousand in profits by selling on etsy.com — enough to sustain his traveling lifestyle in Thailand and India.

Ayngelina Brogan from *Bacon Is Magic* found that employers saw her travel experience as a positive, adding that, "instead of looking like a hobo to employers, I had headhunters reaching out to me because employers wanted innovative people."

Helen, who blogs at *Helen in Wonderlust*, had a similar experience when she left a stable career and a boyfriend at home to travel for an entire year in Africa. When she returned, she got another job and married that boyfriend. She periodically quits jobs, travels, and returns home, always able to find another position.

She attributes this to her work ethic, emphasizing,

I spent most of my free time planning my trip and worked my ass off until the end, never getting into the mentality of "I'm leaving anyway, so I won't put in 100%." I left work on great terms and kept everyone updated about my adventures.

Not long after I returned home, they offered me a job that was better than the one than I'd had before, and I found that the life skills I picked up traveling really helped me grow personally and professionally.

Traveling doesn't have to be a blank space on a résumé. Traveling gives people the opportunity to become better problem-solvers, to get along with others more easily, to develop self-confidence, and to better understand other cultures in this rapidly globalizing world. More and more companies see the value in this kind of life experience.

Nik Kontoulas, founder of Australia-based online media marketing agency EggMobi, told me, "We won't hire anyone who hasn't traveled before. It's an essential part of personal growth, and we see it as an asset in the workplace."

He had just returned from a trip to Malaysia, where we met, and had learned so much by interacting with different cultures that he decided to make international experience part of his criteria when hiring new talent.

Instead of worrying about losing your job prospects and qualifications by traveling, think about what you can do while you travel that will help your résumé overall.

Instead of worrying about losing your job prospects and qualifications by traveling, think about what you can do while you travel that will help your résumé overall. Think about what an employer in your field might be looking for. Are you in finance? Highlight the negotiation skills you picked up haggling. Are you an artist? Offer to paint some murals while you travel. Are you in marketing? Help a local business get on Twitter, or develop their website. Learn a language, develop a new skill. Find ways to make yourself more, rather than less, attractive due to a sabbatical. Then figure out how to word your travel experience in a way that will make your résumé shine rather than appearing as if you went on a carefree vacation.

Here are some ways to showcase your travels on your résumé in order to make your time abroad shine:

- Highlight any volunteer experience, regardless of brevity, that included set hours, working with other cultures, learning a new skill, or great responsibility of some sort.

- Mention any casual work, even if it was just at a hostel or house-sitting (more on that later) that required self-starting qualities and responsibility.

- Emphasize soft skills using language like the following:

— "Learned how to interact and negotiate with people across cultural and language boundaries in over 20 countries"

- "Quickly adapted to fast-changing environments and cultures"
- "Developed problem-solving skills as a solo traveler in completely new environments"
- "Budgeted, planned, and executed 365-day travel plan independently"

Trust in yourself and your abilities enough to take a leap of faith, and put the effort in before, during, and after your trip to ensure that you have something impressive to point to rather than just a beach-bum holiday. A travel gap doesn't have to be a bad thing!

What to Do About Naysayers

Social creatures that we humans are, it's natural that people will worry about your decision to travel. Parents may fear that you'll be completely out of touch, friends might question your sanity, and mere acquaintances might voice their concern about what they perceive as a questionable or even dangerous choice on your part.

It can be pretty disappointing. The people you care about most might be the least supportive. Negativity can come from unexpected places. It starts to seem like everyone has an opinion, from your mother's best friend to the guy who bags your groceries. Even one negative comment in a sea of positivity can rock you if you're not prepared for any and all reactions.

In the days leading up to my departure, a few friends sent me a news article about two girls who had died while traveling in Vietnam, along with the warning, "Be careful!"

The suspected cause of death was drinking poisoned alcohol. The article also mentioned two other deaths in Laos and Thailand over the previous two years that may or may not have been related. While my friends saw warning bells, I was encouraged. Over the course of two years, and in three completely different countries, the number of young female tourist deaths was actually minimal.

(That same week, a crazed moviegoer opened fire in a crowded theater in Colorado. Nobody seemed to notice that, when comparing the two places, I was actually heading somewhere statistically safer than the United States. By moving abroad, I actually lowered my chances of becoming a victim of violent crime.)

How can we get past this? First, get clear on whose opinion really matters.

Brené Brown, professor at the University of Houston Graduate College of Social Work and author of the *New York Times* best-seller *Daring Greatly: How the Courage to Be Vulnerable Transforms the Way We Live, Love, Parent, and Lead*, emphasizes that it's not complete fortitude and confidence in every decision that makes a person achieve great things, but the willingness to be vulnerable, to take negativity from others with a pinch of salt, and to take a chance.

She suggests writing a short list of people whose opinions really matter to you. Whose feedback has aided you in a time of need, and whose advice has helped you move forward in a positive direction? Who really knows you to your core? Anyone who doesn't fit on that very short list can go ahead and give you an opinion about your travels, but that doesn't mean that you have to internalize it.

Quite often the disapproval put forth by others is a result of their own insecurities projected onto you. It may be hard not to focus on that negativity, but all daring dreams come with a willingness to handle some adversity. Consider the valid concerns and come up with plans and answers. Remember that proving them all wrong will make you feel that much more confident and fearless in the end.

For many people, the toughest part is convincing their parents that they'll be all right. A couple of years ago, Alice, a girl who had been working in New York and had dreams of traveling, wrote to me:

The problem is my parents: they are laying the guilt and anxiety on thick whenever I mention the prospect of this trip, and going alone. My mom has shed tears during two out of three quick chats on the subject, and my dad is afraid I will go missing in what he feels is an inaccessible part of the world. I've tried showing them solo blogs, articles, etc., but I'm their only daughter (and only child) and they're nervous. I explained to them that I would love to travel with someone, but it's just not feasible, and I can't delay the trip forever waiting for a friend to come along.

In response I conducted an interview with my mother in order to present the situation from a parent's point of view. My mother laid out the following tips (each followed by my elaboration):

- **Plan it out heavily:** Make it clear that this isn't just some immature idea you have or a scheme to run away from responsibility by planning it out in detail. I did a ton of planning for the trip ahead of me. My mother knows I'm not a planner by nature, so when she realized how much time and thought I'd put into making this life change, it made it clear to her how important it was to me.

- **Highlight past experience:** I had some previous experience studying abroad in Taiwan, so it wasn't my first time doing something that big independently. Have you traveled alone before, even for a weekend? Have you moved across the country, or done something else independently that demonstrates your abilities? Remind them of that. If you don't have experience, go out and get some. Plan a vacation or a weekend away. Gain some experience to speak of.

- **Stay in touch:** Traveling today is not like it was 20 years ago, when most developing countries did not have Wi-Fi and snail mail was the only way to stay in contact. Nowadays infrastructure is improving worldwide and cell phones are ubiquitous. Going off the grid is still possible, but finding easy and free ways to stay in contact is easier now than it has ever been before (more on that later).

- **Remind them that you're capable:** You have a good head on your shoulders. Your parents raised a capable daughter, didn't they? Ask them to trust your intuition and not to hold you back from living out your own dreams.

- **Help them understand that the world is not that scary:** The media works against us big-time by making one death abroad seem like a huge deal, when — compared to the dangers at home (where you are probably often alone) — it's not actually. What's the difference between sitting on a beach in my hometown of Los Angeles or being alone in Thailand? The crime rate, actually, which is higher in Los Angeles.

- **Invite them to join you for a week:** Let your family and friends be part of your journey, if you're willing to share a bit of it with them. It can put them at *ease by being more involved, even if for a short while.*

My mother and I in Zermatt, Switzerland. Each year she visits me for two weeks.

It might not be possible to convince everyone in your circle that your travel plans are a good idea. That's OK. People worry because they love you. However, their opinions will naturally be a buzzkill. When that happens, you just have to remember that this is your life, and your decision.

As for Alice, a year or so passed and she wrote to me again, this time with some wonderful news: *"We chatted last year before I went and traveled around Asia a bit. [I just wanted to let you know that] my trip was FANTASTIC."*

She decided that, despite her parents' worries, she wanted to live out life on her own terms and not to let their fears hold her back. In the end, it worked out, and she proved to everyone, including herself, just how independent and resilient she could be. Just like Alice, you can do the same. Allow yourself to be selfish. Know that it's OK.

How to Build Self-Confidence

I was shaking in my shoes all the way until I landed in Bangkok. That was months and months of nerves plaguing me, mainly because I had no idea what awaited me on the other side of the world. And despite all of the positive things I had read, I still feared what I didn't know.

Yet with fear comes excitement. Hitting the confirmation button when buying that plane ticket will release a surge of emotions — positive, negative, and everything in between.

When fear creeps in, think of all the possibilities, and the fact that every choice is yours to make. Solo travelers never have to agree to go somewhere they don't want to go simply to please someone else. They have the freedom to make last-minute decisions without negatively impacting the travel experience of any friends or family members, because nobody is around to disappoint. Traveling on your own means having the ultimate flexibility and no need to stress about planning out every last detail. Solo travelers can go with the flow.30

Yvonne Zagermann, who left her job as a television producer in Germany at age 31 and now writes the *Just Travelous* blog, agrees, adding,

For me traveling solo is the best way to get to know me better, to get to know my fears, my strengths, and everything in between. I truly enjoy my own company, I enjoy doing whatever the f*** I want, being adventurous, being a chicken. The only person I have to prove myself to is me. And I'm constantly surprised by how adventurous the chicken-hearted me can be when there's no one else to judge.

Think about the times you've overcome difficult things in the past: losing a family member, a significant other, a job, or something else that was of great importance. We've all likely also had an opportunity at some point in our lives to impress ourselves with our own resilience, whether by standing up to the bully in third grade or by bouncing back from a major life crisis.

Solo traveling is yet another opportunity to show everyone — but most importantly yourself — what you're capable of. Even if the fear is still there up until the moment of departure, taking each necessary step toward a solo trip builds confidence bit by bit.

Mountain conquered: Standing atop Mt. Kinabalu in Borneo with two new friends

As Amelia Earhart said in the opening quote of the chapter, the hardest part is not actually acting, but making the decision to act despite all of the fears. The things that society, our loved ones, and the voice inside tend to warn against are things that haven't even happened yet, and likely won't. Sadly these fears keep the vast majority of solo travelers from even taking the first step, which is deciding to go.

When the fears creep in, remember the points from this chapter: there are ways to make the résumé stronger thanks to traveling, the world at large can be even safer than back home, there will always be naysayers, and there are many sources of inspiration out there that can keep you motivated and supported.

If you can get past the fear, or at least learn to deal with it during the process of planning your journey, then the hard part is already behind you. The next steps of saving up money and getting all of your affairs in order prior to your trip are the easy part.

What About Money?: Do What You Can, Then Just Get Out There

"Great people do things before they're ready. They do things before they know they can do it. Doing what you're afraid of, getting out of your comfort zone, taking risks like that, that's what life is. You might be really good. You might find something out about yourself that's really special. And if you're not good, who cares? You tried something. Now you know something about yourself."

—AMY POEHLER, comedian, actress, and cofounder of the improv comedy school The Upright Citizens Brigade Theatre

Apart from getting over your fear and deciding to travel, the most important part of planning a long-term solo trip is the financial aspect of it. Unless you plan to work on the road (which we'll talk more about later), you'll need a healthy sum of cash to support your trip. All too often, the reason why people have to return home from what was supposed to be a much longer trip is because they've run out of cash. The following are steps to help make sure that doesn't happen to you.

How Much Money Do You Really Need?

Part of killing some of the fear of traveling solo has to do with preparation, and having enough money to sustain one's travels is a big part of that. Additionally, having a rainy day fund to use when you return home is essential. Always have a fallback plan.

I put aside $20,000 for my travels, but during my first six-month stint in Southeast Asia, I only spent a total of $7,958 on the ground (meaning not including my flight, travel gear, insurance, and immunizations). Without my expensive scuba diving habit, I would have spent closer to $6,000, averaging $1,000 per month or the "golden" $30 per day.

My budget was achievable by moving slowly, eating and lodging cheaply, and traveling in a part of the world that is inexpensive and easy to get around. What should you budget for your trip? Consider the following factors:

How quickly will you move?

How much of the globe do you want to cover, and how quickly do you aim to move? The more destinations you want to see, the more you'll spend.

Slower movement means buying fewer train, bus, and plane tickets and spending money on fewer visas, all of which can be the most expensive part of traveling. Hopping around South America, for example, where the visa and reciprocity fees top $100 in many countries, quick movement gets very costly. Add that to the $10–$200 you might have spent on a bus or plane journey and the budget is blown quickly.

When I planned my trip, I envisioned a year in Asia, taking very few flights and moving slowly through each country, exploring in such a way that was logical and didn't involve backtracking. Though I deviated from that plan by heading to Australia and New Zealand and returning to Thailand three times that first year, the months that I spent in just one country, moving slowly, were the cheapest.

If your budget won't allow for a trip that covers the globe, don't despair. Moving slowly does not necessarily mean seeing less. On the contrary, it will give you a better chance to get to know the area you're traveling through on a deeper level.

Where will you go?

The area of the world matters quite a bit when planning a budget. Australia, New Zealand, Japan, Canada, the United States, and Western Europe (especially Scandinavian countries) all rank pretty high in terms of costs associated with eating, sleeping, getting around, and sightseeing. For example, a plate with only eggs and toast in Melbourne costs around AUD $12 ($9.40 USD) and a nonpremium beer at a bar is around $10 ($7.80 USD). This is standard in most of Australia and not easy to stomach when living only off of savings.

The next tier includes many of the countries on the African continent, China, Taiwan, South Korea, Singapore, Eastern Europe, the Caribbean, and Russia. These places often have one or two cheap aspects, such as food or in some cases lodging, but it can also get pricey in other aspects. My budget for South Africa, for example, was $56 per day due to the high costs of transport and activities, even though food was affordable, the exchange rate was in my favor, and I often had free accommodation by staying with friends.

The last tier includes the rest of the developing world. Most of Southeast Asia, India, Nepal, most of Central America, and much of South America (with a few exceptions, such as Brazil, Chile, and the city of Buenos Aires) are generally much friendlier on a backpacker budget, and the cost of just about everything — food, accommodation, and transportation — is lower than in any Western country.

Let's consider my daily budget in cheap Cambodia vs. expensive Iceland:

Cambodia – $13/day and up:

- **Food and drink:** $10–15: Eggs and a baguette for breakfast with tea, curry for lunch, and a freshly caught fish with rice and salad for dinner with a $1 beer.

- **Hostel:** $2–6: Dorms in Cambodia are dirt-cheap!

- **Activities:** $0–40: The most expensive things I did in Cambodia were buying a ticket to Angkor Wat and splitting a tuk-tuk with a dorm-mate, or going scuba diving.

- **Transport:** $1–15: Depending on distance and how many people I could split with, transport ranged from $1 for my share of a tuk-tuk around town to $15 for a long-distance bus.

Iceland – $93/day and up

- **Food and drink:** $30–100: Buying food at grocery stores and cooking it yourself will help to save some money, but even a gas station sandwich in Iceland costs $10 and up! A beer costs about the same.

- **Hostel:** $30–60: Accommodation is also a big part of the costs in Iceland; however, if you camp during low season, it's free!

- **Activities:** $0–200: The great thing about Iceland is once you have accommodation and transport sorted out, most sightseeing is free. Tours like snorkeling, whale watching, and scenic helicopter flights, however, cost about the same as they would in the US and the rest of Europe.

- **Transport:** $35–200: During high season, 4x4 camper van rentals can get quite expensive, so try to share with a fellow traveler if possible. Sad Car rentals in the capital of Reykjavik can be as low as $30/day, plus gas.

As you can see from the comparison, your money in Cambodia will go a lot farther. Take this into consideration when you decide where in the world you want to go, and for how long.

Where will you sleep?

Accommodation is right up there with plane flights as one of the largest parts of the travel budget. Private rooms almost always cost more, and as a solo traveler, this will usually mean spending on a double occupancy rate for just one person. Are you willing to stay in dorms? If so, you'll be able to save a lot of money and meet people easily in the process.

If having your own space is important, go back to the previous point and think about which part of the world you wish to travel through. A private beach bungalow in Goa, India, will cost less than $10 per day, but sky's the limit for a beach bungalow in Hawaii. We'll touch on this more in the last section of this chapter.

Which activities will you spend your money on?

As I mentioned earlier, I have an expensive scuba diving habit. During my Southeast Asia trip, I racked up over 80 dives — and it wasn't cheap. In order to afford it and to travel for longer, I stayed almost exclusively in dorms for nearly two years and only ate street food. I was happy to do it because I love diving (and street food) that much.

Other activities I love, like a day at the beach or going for a walk or hike, are usually free. By balancing out expensive and cheap activities, I got the full travel experience.

Think about what you want to do in the places you visit and devote at least 30% of your budget to that. Too many travelers spend their money elsewhere and leave nothing for activities. I watched as they missed out on amazing things, such as visiting Angkor Wat in Cambodia or bungee jumping in South Africa, because they didn't factor it into their budget. You didn't plan the trip of a lifetime to only miss out on the actual joy of traveling, right?

Will you travel on a shoestring budget or do you seek affordable luxury?

There are quite a few discomforts I put up with during my time in Southeast Asia. If I had the option of saving money by taking an overnight bus instead of a flight, I did. If I could save a few dollars by sleeping in a dorm with a fan instead of air conditioning, I opted for the fan. I only took public transportation with locals, while most tourists traveled in private tourist vans or boats. Those little daily concessions made it possible to achieve a budget of $30 per day.

Think about what makes you happy as a traveler and budget accordingly. Decide what kind of accommodation, transport, and food you're comfortable with and what part of the world you most want to see. Be honest with yourself about what you can handle and save up accordingly.

If you're the budget type, Matt Kepnes literally wrote the book on the subject: *How to Travel the World on $50 a Day*. If you're not, then rein in your expectations of how far your money will go, or pick a cheaper destination.

Also consider that as a solo traveler, costs are a bit higher, unfortunately. It seems like it should be half the cost of traveling as a couple, but sadly it isn't even close. Though you will most definitely meet other people to split costs with from time to time, there will be destinations where there are no hostel dorm beds and you'll have to pay for a hotel room for one, or you'll arrive in a city solo and have to shoulder an entire taxi fare or a single supplement for a tour you want to take (though thankfully, according to New York Times travel columnist Stephanie Rosenbloom, more and more tour companies are scrapping that extra charge as solo travel becomes more popular).

Regardless of your travel style, it's still a good idea to track what you're spending on a daily basis. That way, if you start going over budget, you'll see exactly what's causing it (spoiler alert: it's usually alcohol and partying).

Saving Up: The 50/30/20 Rule

The best way to start a savings plan is to truly understand everything you spend your money on. To calculate that, keep a meticulous record of your spending habits, day by day, over the course of a month. It's tedious, but it works and will show you where your money really goes. Your findings may surprise you! Many of the things that seem essential can probably be cut out, and recognizing where the real expenses lie can make saving up a bit easier, though it will require discipline.

A great metric for spending is the 50/30/20 rule, invented by Harvard law professor, bankruptcy expert, and US senator Elizabeth Warren and her daughter Amelia Warren Tyagi in their book *All Your Worth: The Ultimate Lifetime Money Plan* as an ideal rule for budgeting. The idea is that

50% of your income goes toward needs, 30% toward wants, and 20% toward savings.

To calculate this, first determine your after-tax income. If you're an employee, taxes are most likely already taken out of your paycheck. Add back in any deductions, such as healthcare or retirement contributions that you make yourself, just as you would if preparing your taxes. If you're an independent contractor or self-employed, subtract your business expenses and tax liability from your gross income. What you are left with is what you can use for the 50/30/20 breakdown.

Next, write down your needs, i.e., every necessary life expense you have. What this should include is not as easy to calculate as it seems on the surface, but it comes down to anything that would severely limit your quality of life if it were missing or that simply must be paid monthly. This includes:

- *Rent or mortgage payments*
- *Utilities such as electricity and water*
- *Insurance*
- *Healthcare premiums and expenses*
- *Retirement contributions*
- *School loan payments*
- *Credit card payments*
- *Car payments*
- *Phone bills*
- *Groceries, and any other bills that would harm your credit score if not handled on a monthly basis*

You can use Mint or a similar service to keep track of and categorize your spending.

The tricky category is the "wants" category. At first 30% for wants sounds great! How about those awesome stilettos? Or joining that expensive yoga studio? Hello, Vegas weekend!

In reality, anything that would cause a minor inconvenience, such as cable TV or having a car in a city with public transportation, is more of a want than a need. An unlimited cell phone data plan, shopping at a more expensive grocery store (or buying more expensive food items), choosing restaurants over cooking at home, and even buying clothing beyond what is required for work or general survival is a "want," not a "need."

Cut down on "wants"

*   **Beverages:** If you live in a country where tap water is drinkable (and you probably do), switch to filtered tap water and ditch bottled water. If you are addicted to Starbucks or a similar coffee shop, break the habit now! Add up how much that daily coffee costs, and chances are that over the course of a year, you'll have enough to buy a few plane tickets. Get a French press and brew your own cup for way less with coffee from the grocery store.

*   **Television:** Get rid of cable TV. For most households, this expense represents over $100 per month. Besides, most things can be watched online for free these days or friend's place (or at a restaurant if we're talking sporting events).

- **Cell phone:** Scale way back on that cell phone plan. Unlimited 4G certainly is nice, but read a book instead of streaming YouTube videos on your phone and you could save $50+ monthly on your phone bill.

- **Entertainment:** Think about all of the things that you could do for entertainment value that cost little or no money. Could dinners out be replaced by a picnic in the park with food you've cooked yourself and would eat anyway? Wouldn't a bike ride be a nice alternative to a movie? Most cities and even small towns have loads of free activities worth taking advantage of. Saving money doesn't have to mean leading a boring life.

- **Retail therapy:** Shopping is fun. Buying new clothing that fits like a glove and killer shoes to go with is certainly gratifying, but only temporarily. Each $200 dress equates to about a week's worth of adventures in many countries abroad. In that context, is it really worth looking good for just a few hours out? Nope! For clothes that are completely necessary, such as for work, look at secondhand stores first.

Saving money often comes down to one's mentality. Working in a rewards system every time you save another dollar here or there can make it fun rather than torturous. A great way to make it into a game is to select an exciting travel expense, like a diving certification or a retreat that you really want to attend, and make a little poster that you color in little by little with each dollar that you save towards that activity. It can make the savings process gratifying rather than grueling.

Of course it's natural to still give into the occasional want, but it must be done much less often. Going out and partying is easily one of the biggest budget eaters, both at home and when traveling. Even cheap drinks add up over time, as do transportation for your night out, door entry fees, and even the associated recovery time that could be spent working and earning instead.

Pick and choose the events that you really need to go to, and cut out any that aren't essential to maintaining friendships (such as birthday parties) or networking. Partying less doesn't have to mean being less social, though. Invite friends over and do potluck house parties or movie nights instead. Everyone benefits from the added savings and equal amount of socializing.

Next, reevaluate the "needs" category

There are various methods of cutting expenses, such as learning to cook, that can save a lot of money over time:

- **Food:**

— Look at some of your favorite snacks and cereals and compare the cost to buying apples or raw meats and grains instead, and you might be pretty surprised at the difference.

— Breaking up shopping between several stores also helps. By shopping at farmers' markets and dedicated produce outlets weekly, veggie costs go way down; when cooking with raw ingredients, they make up a big portion of most recipes. Saving money takes more time and effort, but the reward of traveling is worth it.

- **Cooking habits:**

— Search online for recipes that are designed to cost less than $10. This usually means using raw rather than processed ingredients, which will be healthier anyways — it's snack food and easy meals that cost the most. Cheap food can still be full of great flavors and the nutrients you need, and cooking is quite fun once you get the hang of it and find recipes that you like.

— Cook when you have free time, save the leftovers, and rather than buying a meal on the go because you're out of food and time, you'll have something already waiting for you at home or in your lunch box.

— Think about investing in _ Apmai +Nmr. Throw the ingredients in, let it cook during the day, and come home to a delicious, slow-cooked meal.

- **Rent:**

— Try to cut out rent completely. Move in with family members or find some other rent-free situation. I know it's not fun moving back home as an adult, but doing so saved me nearly $1,400 per month!

— Consider getting a roommate. If moving in with family members isn't an option for you, or if you can be mobile, move somewhere cheaper and deal with a smaller place or less desirable location leading up to your departure. Accommodation is such a big part of the needs category, so cut it as much as you can.

- **Transportation:**

— In Southern California, with its practically nonexistent public transportation options, I did still need my car but put more effort into finding others to share the expense, and I carpooled a lot more.

— If biking, walking, or taking the train are options where you live, go for that. Cutting out a car, with its attendant gas costs and insurance payments, can save hundreds per month. If not, only drive when necessary or carpool and share the cost of gas.

If possible, try to switch around the equation: spend 30% on needs, 20% on wants (which should go toward things like a camera or travel gear for your trip), and 50% on savings. Continue to keep meticulous records of your spending, on a daily basis if you have to, in order to keep yourself in check and to make sure that you're on target with your percentages.

Finding Ways to Earn More Before You Go

There are even more little things you can do to save a dollar here or earn one there, and they're surprisingly easy:

Fill out surveys

I filled out online surveys for a few years leading up to my departure. They didn't pay in cash, but they did compensate with gift cards. This way, I could still purchase clothing for my work wardrobe, which was a need, but I was only spending my time to replenish my wardrobe, not my money.

For a couple of years, I was able to earn about $50 in gift cards every other month. Therefore I was able to put toward my trip the money I would otherwise have spent replacing threadbare polo shirts.

The key was to respond as quickly as possible when they sent out an email since the surveys only need a finite number of responses.

Run your own small group tours

Thanks to companies like *Vayable, Voyagin,* and *Guide Me Right,* you can now be a tour guide, run your own group tours, and offer travelers an authentic and localized experience from where you live. Doing this also allows you to expand your network and meet people from countries you may plan to visit in the future. Killing two birds with one stone here, really.

Tap into the sharing economy

The sharing economy is based on the principle that excess products or various services can be traded directly between providers and seekers by utilizing technology for communication.

Do you have a skill that can be put to use in your community? Advertise your handyman, house cleaning, or even baking abilities on services like *Craigslist* and *Gumtree*, or *Zaarly*. There are also online marketplaces that allow you to offer digital marketing, designing, or programming services, such as *Fiverr* and *Freelancer*, to companies around the world.

Is there a spare room in your house that can be rented out for some extra income each month? Take a look at *Airbnb*, which allows renters to lease out their entire homes or just a room for a few days to vacationers passing through. If you can't get out of your lease, stay with friends every now and then and rent out your place in order to subsidize your rent. Have a private parking space? Rent it out via *ParqEx* (US) or *JustPark* (UK).

For those who don't need a car on a daily basis, look into ridesharing options like *Getaround.com*, which allows short-term peer-to-peer car rentals. That way if you get rid of your car, you still have options, and if you keep your car, you can rent it out on the weekends or times when you don't need it. Also look into providing rides through apps like *Lyft* and *Zipcar* to help ease the financial burden of owning a car.

Get rid of furniture

I moved out of my mother's house when I was 18, and ever since then I've accumulated various items of furniture and knick-knacks. By the time I made the decision to start traveling, there was eight years of accumulated stuff to get rid of. Some of it was sentimental, and if it was small enough, I kept it. Most of it, however, was big items like couches and tables, IKEA stuff that I had bought secondhand, but it still looked good and was in great condition.

The week before the lease on my apartment ended and I prepared to move back to my mother's place, I sold every last item of furniture I owned on *Craigslist*, with most pieces going for $30–80 (if you're in the UK or Australia, the equivalent is *Gumtree*; in Canada, *Kijiji* is also a great option). If your furniture is more expensive, consider if it's worth taking a loss on the sale price in order to save on storage costs.

A week wasn't much time to sell everything, but I had a system for selling quickly, and it worked like a charm:

First, check out the general pricing for the items you want to sell by looking at existing ads. Chances are there will be a lot of very similar items and the competition will be stiff.

In order to sell quickly, undercut the competition by just a few dollars here and there, which makes your items more appealing and the selling process quicker. Even though I know my stuff could probably have fetched a little over what I was asking, it was worth it in order to sell it all quickly rather than having to figure out how to haul it away or store it.

Next comes the marketing — and this is where some ads really stand out and others disappear into the endless listings abyss. Most people on Craigslist take horrible pictures of their items, and they come across looking cheap and unappealing. When scanning through a list of items quickly, what's going to stand out? A great tagline and an even better photo will every time.

Take photos of the items during daylight hours and edit them so that they look fabulous, even if it's just a smartphone photo edited with an app like *Camera Plus* or *Snapseed*. Include multiple angles if that helps your cause. A bit of staging with a nice plant or beautiful lamp never hurts, either.

Next, make the tagline pop. Simply using adjectives like "beautiful," "chic," and "comfortable" in taglines will get people clicking. Then keep it very short and to the point and informative. Include item measurements and pickup requirements. Answer any obvious questions in the posting, so that your email inbox doesn't get bogged down with people seeking information.

To kick it up a notch, I even included "Selling everything I own to travel — your purchase helps me travel longer" in each post. This humanized me and made people interested in my story. As an added benefit, almost nobody haggled with me, a rarity on Craigslist.

Not getting hits right away? Delete and repost the item within 12–24 hours at a lower price. Try another photo. This takes some effort, but ultimately the $40 here and there will add up and, even better, cuts all of your moving costs, since people come and pick up the items themselves.

Finally, the most important point is to be available. Internet buyers are flaky. They'll ask to meet at 10 a.m. and won't show up until 2 p.m. It's annoying, but it's part of the process. Try to be home as much as possible that week, and do your selling during daylight hours. If you live solo like I did at the time, give the nearest cross streets and ask sellers to call you when they arrive; then go outside to meet them, just to make sure that the buyers are serious and so that you're not giving out your exact address.

Have stuff that won't sell on Craigslist? If you've slashed the price yet can't find a buyer, ask the *Salvation Army* or a similar organization in your area to pick it up if you can't drop it off yourself. This is one of the few organizations I was able to find that would do this without a compulsory monetary donation or fee. Plus, it's a tax-deductible donation.

Part with excess clothing and electronics

How much is coming with you on your trip? I'd suggest a week to a week and a half's worth of items at most (but more on that later). I had a walk-in closet full of clothing, some of which my mother has been kind enough to let me store at her place, if I'm honest — there are some things like a pretty purse or that favorite pair of boots that a girl just can't part with! As for the rest, I did have to get honest with myself about what I really needed and so got rid of a lot of stuff before I left.

This can be a painful process, but you don't necessarily have to give it all away — you can sell it! Go through your closets and be ruthless. What haven't you worn in a year? What doesn't really fit anymore? Take the excess clothing that is still in good condition (and especially designer) and try selling it to thrift and consignment stores. They're choosy, tend to make selections based on the season, and only provide pennies on the dollar for the original sale price, but it's cash in hand and better than simply giving your clothing away:

- **United States:** *Check Crossroads Trading Company and the Buffalo Exchange, both of which will take higher-end clothing.*

- **Canada:** *Check out Cash 4 Clothes or Trend Trunk in each major city.*

- **United Kingdom:** *Options include Return to Earn and Music and Goods Exchange in a few major areas, which take all kinds of used items.*

- **Australia:** *Check out Blue Spinach in Sydney and Secondo in Melbourne.*

- **Online:** *Poshmark and ThredUP are options for selling everything from less expensive to premium brands online and through their smartphone app. They currently operate in the United States but are in the process of expanding internationally.*

Have electronics you want to get rid of so that you can upgrade for your trip? Take a look at *USell*, which mainly deals in phones and other electronics but even has categories for textbooks.

It may seem sad at first to get rid of your belongings, but the thrill of the deal, feeling lighter with each item squared away, and thinking of all the experiences you will be able to afford because of the money in your pocket will ease the sting. That sweater you haven't worn in two years can earn you ten plates of pad thai!

Prepping Like a Boss: *Planning Made Manageable*

"Courage is more exhilarating than fear, and in the long run it is easier. We do not have to become heroes overnight. Just a step at a time, meeting each thing that comes up, seeing it is not as dreadful as it appeared, discovering we have the strength to stare it down."

—ELEANOR ROOSEVELT, from her book You Learn By Living

Now it's time to get into the nitty-gritty of how much (or how little) to plan out your itinerary. This chapter explores how to best tie up loose ends, leave bridges intact rather than burning them, and find a way to intelligently move forward.

Itinerary Planning

How much time should be spent on planning out an itinerary? This is an area of confusion — and sometimes stress — for a lot of solo travelers. How much should be planned ahead when all of the decisions fall to you?

I am not a planner by nature. I did a lot of budgeting and pre-trip prep, but as for my actual itinerary, I completely winged it. As in, I didn't even have a hostel booked for my first night in Bangkok. I just showed up and found something I liked by walking door to door and checking out the rooms, and then picking something that fit my budget. I only bought the one-way ticket and figured that the rest would work itself out — and it did.

The beauty is that as a solo traveler, you have the flexibility of being able to change your mind without it impacting anyone else. For example, you may desire to stay longer in some places or less time in others than you initially thought. Perhaps you'll meet someone who you want to stick with for longer, and that will change your plans entirely. Perhaps you'll end up really disliking a place you thought you'd love, or will love a place you knew nothing about back in the planning stages and will want to stay longer.

During my first month of travels in Cambodia, I met an Argentinian named Julián, who had arrived in Otres Beach, a coastal town with a sleepy vibe and cheap digs, for the same reason that I had: word of mouth (it wasn't in any guidebooks back then). He stayed for a month in the same shared hostel room, bought fruit from the same lady each day, and drank a nightly 50-cent beer at the one and only open-air pub. He eventually got a casual job there, all because he loved it so much that he wanted to stay longer. Had he made rigid plans for himself, he would not have been able to extend his stay.

Not everyone can handle that kind of uncertainty, though.

Louise, an American who bases herself in Buenos Aires doing freelance virtual assistant work, says that she is a planner by nature, but in order to allow some spontaneity in her solo trip, she planned to have a chunk of time that would be unplanned. It sounds like an oxymoron, but she intentionally forced herself to leave some room in her itinerary that had nothing booked and nothing decided, just to get out of her comfort zone a bit and to allow for improvisation.

Jo Fitzsimons, former London-based lawyer turned solo female travel blogger, is on the far end of the planning spectrum:

I was a frantic planner before I went traveling so it was no surprise I planned my trip to within an inch of its life. I read every page of The Rough Guide to First-Time Around the World by Doug Lansky (a book I'd still recommend), and I had spreadsheets and lists coming out of my ears. But still, it helped me calm my nerves. When I'd ticked off (almost) everything on my to-do list, I knew there was nothing else but to just go out there and travel. You may overplan, you'll probably overpack, but if it helps you get from dreaming to doing, then it's all worth it.

She purchased a round-the world (hereafter abbreviated RTW) ticket, which left little flexibility in her schedule for any changes, and happily stuck to it.

In order to plan out your itinerary (or not), take the following steps:

- Ask yourself how much spontaneity you enjoy.

- Look at distances between places to see how much you can realistically cover in your given time frame.

- Select a method of transport (Planes or trains? How much time do you have to cover said distances?).

- Evaluate itinerary desires against budget capabilities.

- Look up and understand visa requirements for all countries under consideration.

- Buy a ticket (maybe an RTW ticket?).

Flights

That brings me to flights. Is an RTW ticket the right choice for you? If you are just traveling in a particular region and covering short distances, there's no need to think about RTW tickets. In this case, buying a one-way ticket or a point-to-point ticket will make more sense. If you're unsure of your end date or where you'll fly out of, you may want to opt for a one-way. However, this is almost always more expensive.

For example, when I flew to Bangkok, I planned on staying in Southeast Asia for a while, moving slowly throughout that region to save money. I didn't know exactly when I would return to the US or from where, so I waited and bought a one-way ticket home from Vietnam later in the year. In hindsight, I should have just bought a round-trip ticket to save money. It wouldn't have been that expensive to get back to a major hub like Bangkok from elsewhere within Southeast Asia, and I probably would have saved at least $100.

If I had wanted to cover many points all over the globe, especially for a fixed amount of time, buying an RTW ticket and planning everything up front could have saved me a bit of money. However, these tickets leave almost no room for flexibility or itinerary changes.

Lily Leung, who formerly worked in corporate America, wrote in her travel blog *Explore for a Year* that she spent around $3,600 for all of her flights without purchasing an RTW ticket ahead of time. She reports that it ended up being the same overall price as what she was quoted for an RTW ticket. She chose to purchase her flights separately for several reasons:

- RTW tickets cannot be modified without a lot of headache and extra expense, if at all.
- She didn't want to have to decide everything for a full year of traveling in advance
- Regional and low-cost airlines are not part of the major airline alliances that provide such flight packages.

What about planning ahead, though? That depends on which part of the world you're traveling in.

Trains, buses, and ferries in Southeast Asia are cheap, and there's no penalty for buying at the last minute or even showing up at the bus depot and buying the day of. AirAsia flights are also super cheap, as was the case with my $18 ticket from Kuala Lumpur in peninsular Malaysia to Kota Kinabalu in Malaysian Borneo, purchased two weeks prior to departure. I got this low fare by signing up for the airline's newsletter and scanning sales each time they emailed. Booking flights with regional airlines in South Africa is also not a problem, where a same-day flight from Johannesburg to Durban with Kulula Airlines can be purchased for $60 one-way, even in the middle of their summer.

However, last-minute planning in other parts of the world can have expensive consequences. In Europe, trains and planes booked closer to the date of travel tend to go up quite a bit in price. The same is generally true in the United States and Canada.

Long-haul flights are similar in this regard and are ideally booked about two months in advance, though the jury is out on exactly when the best time to book is and how to get the lowest possible fares. Flexibility usually comes at an expense in these cases, and some planning ahead is necessary to ease the pressure on the bank account.

How much planning and purchasing ahead of time you wish to do comes down to where in the world you want to go, how quickly you plan to move, and how much of the globe you aim to cover. It also has to do with your personality type and how much spontaneity you enjoy. If planning everything out helps ease your mind, then do it. If it doesn't, then don't.

How to find a cheap ticket that works for you

Whether you opt for an RTW ticket that allows you to hit multiple parts of the world during your journey, or prefer a point-to-point ticket that gets you out and back home, these tips will help you get a ticket for less:

How to find cheap point-to-point tickets:

Step 1: Be flexible.

If you can be flexible with your departure date and where you fly into first, you can save a lot of money. If you are dead-set on visiting Paris, for example, go to Paris in the spring or fall when fewer people visit and airfares are cheaper.

Moreover, it's cheaper to fly during the middle of the week than on a weekend, because most people travel on the weekends and airlines hike their prices then. The difference of one day can mean hundreds of dollars in savings. Prices are also cheaper if you take the less-than-desirable times, like in the early morning or late at night.

Airline search engines have made it really easy to search the entire world to find the cheapest ticket — you no longer have to search manually. Kayak offers the "Explore" tool that allows you to put in your home airport and see a map of the world with all of the flight options on it. Google Flights also has a similar feature. If you are flexible with where you want to go (you can even choose "anywhere but home"), you can often score quite a deal. These are wonderful tools to start your planning with.

Step 2: Consider budget airlines.

I mentioned earlier that one-way tickets are often more expensive, but that's not actually the case with most budget airlines, like Norwegian or Southwest, who price all of their fares as one-way flights.

I once scored a flight from Los Angeles to Copenhagen for $196 on Norwegian, and have seen WOW Air offer flights to Iceland for less than $300 from San Francisco.

Remember that these airlines almost always charge a lot for extras like checked bags and meals on board. If you're traveling carry-on only and bring food from home, that's no big deal, but if you want to check a bag or two, make sure it's worth it.

The best budget airlines are Southwest, Spirit, Ryanair, WOW, Norwegian, Tiger Airways, Flydubai, and AirAsia. Apart from Southwest, these options all show up on Google Flights.

Step 3: Try flying into a major hub first.

Let's say you're dying to visit Berlin, but it's much cheaper to fly into London first. If you have the time to be flexible, consider flying into London, spending a few hours or days there, and then flying a budget regional airline into Berlin.

If I do this, I try to leave a buffer of at least a day or two just in case my international flight is delayed. If you don't leave enough time for a delay or cancellation, you could get stuck buying a new onward regional flight. Leave plenty of time just in case!

Step 4: Check across several search engines.

Search as many flight search websites as you can in order to ensure you are leaving no stone unturned. Many search sites don't list budget carriers because those airlines don't want to pay a booking commission, while others don't list booking sites that aren't in English.

It's important to check a few sites before you book, as you'll often see variations in prices, and you don't want to miss a deal. The best search engines are the ones that have no affiliation with any airline and make their money via advertising, not bookings. But all websites have their weaknesses and do not include every airline. Here are a few good ones:

- ~~Adioso~~
- **Momondo**
- **Google Flights (this is also the best site for searching multiple cities)**
- **ITA Matrix**
- **Skyscanner**
- **Kayak**

Step 5: Change up the currency and location.

I once found a great flight deal from Berlin to South Africa on Expedia via a search engine, Adioso. Once I switched the currency to USD and the language to English, the price shot way up.

I decided to use the Google Chrome browser, which gives you the option to translate foreign languages, book on the German site in German, and pay in euros. Since I used a travel credit card (more on those later), I didn't get hit with a currency conversion fee, so it was fine. By booking on Expedia.de, I saved about $200. It's worth checking if your flight could be cheaper by changing your browsing destination to the departure or arrival city. You can usually do that on the top right of the browser window.

Step 6: Consider travel hacking.

Over the past year, I haven't had to purchase any of my flights outright, even though I've flown between the US and Europe several times, have flown within Europe, and even purchased a business-class ticket to Chiang Mai from Berlin for just $150.

I did this by travel hacking. I sign up for credit cards that have compelling sign-up bonuses, put every single expense I have on the card, from gas and groceries to online purchases, and pay it off in full every month. I'm careful never to spend beyond what I normally would, and never to overextend myself or carry a balance. Each time I get the bonus, I call and downgrade to a card with no annual fee, and start over again with a new card and compelling offer.

The key is to make sure that you're likely to hit the minimum spend, which might be something like $3,000 within the first three months. If you have a big purchase or the holidays coming up, make that the time that you open the credit card.

Hardcore travel hackers even take this a step further by only shopping at or dining at restaurants that are part of their card's rewards scheme, or doing things like buying gift cards at a retailer that the card offers extra points for and then using the gift card to pay for thing they would have used the card for (that's an old technique that doesn't work anymore, but it's an example of what people do to travel hack).

I've never gone to extremes, but I have been able to fly for cheap or free thanks to my mileage points.

I talk more about travel credit cards later on in this section, but for those of you who want to get deeper into travel hacking, I recommend sites like *The Points Guy* and Nomadic Matt's *Ultimate Guide to Travel Hacking*. It's a topic that has many nuances and tricks that are constantly changing, and it's enough to fill a book in and of itself!

How to find cheap RTW tickets:

RTW tickets are actually airline alliance passes. You buy a ticket from one airline that can be used with them and their partners. An airline alliance is a partnership in which airlines share seats on planes, passengers, and elite status benefits. For example, if you book with United Airlines (Star Alliance), your ticket is only good for airlines United partners with in that alliance. If you book with American Airlines (Oneworld), you can only use their partners. Since American Airlines can't fly everywhere in the world and you may need to get from New York City to Nairobi, Kenya, a destination American itself doesn't serve, you may book with American Airlines for that route, but you will actually fly one of its airline partners on the portions American doesn't fly.

It's important to remember that none of these alliances include the world's budget airlines such as Ryanair (Europe), Southwest (US), AirAsia (Asia), or Tiger (Asia/ Australia). These usually offers fewer amenities (think cattle car) and cheaper fares than the "major" airlines of the world (i.e., large, international carriers that are part of an alliance), so using them often works out cheaper than any other way to fly.

RTW tickets prices range between $2,700 and $10,000 USD, depending on your mileage, route, and number of stops, though a simple two- or three-stop RTW ticket might cost as little as $1,500 USD.

On all tickets, you can change the dates and times on the ticket at no extra charge so long as you don't change the destinations. If you have a Tokyo-to-Los Angeles flight you want to change, you can change the date and time without a fee. However, if you decide to fly from Tokyo to San Francisco instead then you have to pay a fee (around $125 USD).

While you can book RTW tickets directly with the airlines by calling the reservations line listed on their websites, you can find a better deal by booking through a third party such as AirTreks, STA Travel, or Flight Centre (Australia/NZ). Third-party bookers don't just deal with one alliance, they mix and match from all available airlines (excluding budget airlines) to find the lowest price, which saves you money. Moreover, you can fly anywhere and in any direction you want and the overland mileage doesn't count against your flight because there is no mileage limit.

Health: Where, What, and How?

How will you handle things like immunizations, your healthcare plans at home, and health insurance? This section will help you figure it out step by step.

All of the following information is based on my own experiences and what I found out from my research. **This section does not replace the advice and experience of a trained medical professional.**

Immunizations

Immunizations are one of those pre-trip expenses that are annoying but important and in some cases even required. For example, if you travel to South Africa from Tanzania, they'll probably ask to see your vaccination record. For traveling to countries with yellow fever, a yellow, signed and stamped World Health Organization booklet is often required at borders in order to gain entry.

For travel to anywhere at all, it's advisable to be up to date on your tetanus; hepatitis A and B; and measles, mumps, and rubella (MMR) shots. Tetanus is a dirtborne illness due to cuts or open wounds, hepatitis A is transmitted through contaminated food, and hepatitis B through bodily fluids. In most cases, you may have already had some or all of these immunizations and only need a booster shot. Check your immunization records to be sure. In the United States, private insurance often covers these immunizations.

For much of the world, immunization against typhoid is necessary, which protects against a specific bacterial infection, and for parts of Africa and South America so is immunization against yellow fever, which is transmitted through the bite of a mosquito. In the case of the typhoid vaccine, there is a pill and a jab option. These are typically considered elective in the United States and therefore not covered by most private HMO insurance.

In order to get the cheapest possible vaccinations in the United States and most other countries, visit the travel doctor at the local healthcare clinic rather than your general practitioner, since most insurance will not cover certain travel immunizations. Verify this first with your insurance just to be sure.

Keep in mind that if you go this route, the appointment needs to be made quite in advance, and in some cases an appointment for antimalaria pills (see below) will have to be separate from the immunizations. It is recommended to get most immunizations two months ahead of your departure, except for the hepatitis A shot, which can be had right up to your departure date.

A typical visit to a travel doctor involves discussing the areas you plan to visit; the doctor will then look up and suggest vaccines based on your destinations. Which immunizations you elect to get are up to you.

Your doctor may also suggest getting the rabies vaccine. The cost varies from place to place, but in the United States, it runs about $900 as of September 2017 for the full three-shot series. It does not prevent you from needing another shot if you get bitten; it simply buys you time if you're in a rural area. If you think you might be in a situation where you could be bitten, such as volunteering with animals or hiking in rural areas with monkeys, consider getting the injections.

Antimalarial pills are a topic of some debate in the travel community due to the side effects and the fact that they can't provide 100% protection. There are two types medication meant to help aid in the prevention of malaria: the antibiotic prophylactic doxycycline, and parasite inhibitor combination pill (atovaquone and proguanil), known commercially as Malarone. Doxycycline is cheaper but must be taken for a full month after leaving the malaria zone in order to remain effective. Malarone needs to be taken for only a week after and is known for having fewer side effects. Both, however, have sometimes-severe side effects that should be taken into consideration.

For Canadians, the cost of vaccines depends on which province you live in and which vaccines you get. According to the Public Health Agency of Canada, vaccines are given in doctors' offices or public clinics (or CLSCs in Quebec); for travel-specific vaccines, "you may need to visit a special travel clinic. In most cases, you will need to pay for travel vaccines." The Public Health Agency of Canada's Travel Health Fact Sheet details every disease that can be transmitted on the road, what the symptoms are, and prevention methods.

For UK citizens, according to the National Health Service (NHS) website, the best method for getting travel vaccines is as follows:

First, phone or visit your GP or practice nurse to find out whether your existing UK jabs are up-to-date (they can tell from your notes). Your GP or practice nurse may also be able to give you general advice about travel vaccinations and travel health, such as protecting yourself from malaria. Your GP or practice nurse can give you a booster of your UK jabs if you need one. They may be able to give you the travel jabs you need, either free on the NHS or for a charge. Alternatively, you can visit a local private travel vaccination clinic for your UK boosters and other travel jabs. Not all vaccinations are available free on the NHS, even if they're recommended for travel to a certain area.

The site goes on to say that vaccinations for cholera; typhoid; diphtheria, polio and tetanus (combined booster); and in some cases hepatitis A are free, while vaccinations for meningitis, tuberculosis, rabies (£120–170 for the course of three doses, as opposed to $1,000 in the United States), and yellow fever are paid out of pocket. Yellow fever vaccines are also only available at certain clinics.

For Australians, according to the Australian Department of Health website, appointments with general practitioners should be made 6–8 weeks prior to departure, and travel vaccines generally do need to be paid for out of pocket. Yellow fever vaccines must be obtained at specific clinics.

For Kiwis, apart from those routine immunizations that are free, travel vaccinations are not generally free and must be purchased through your general practitioner, according to the NZ immunization handbook. You can also go to a travel doctor for specific needs like yellow fever.

For everyone else, check with your government's travel advisory and immunizations websites in order to find out what is free, what costs extra, and how to get it in the cheapest way possible. In some cases, such as my visit to southern and eastern Africa, it made more sense for me to wait until arriving in Johannesburg to get my yellow fever vaccination and malaria tablets rather than obtaining both in Europe, where it would have been more expensive and the exchange rate was not in my favor.

As for your health insurance back home, if you're paying for it out of pocket, it may be best to get rid of it. Since most Americans have private healthcare that only covers them domestically, there's not much benefit to keeping and paying for the service while traveling long term. However if you are only on a short trip, you will want to retain healthcare so as not to be penalized (**Note on Obamacare:** *If you don't file taxes in the US, or you are living outside the US for more than 330 days in 12 months, you are automatically exempt.*)

For Canadians, the regulations vary by province, but if you plan to be gone for more than six months, you should contact your province's healthcare plan to discuss your options. UK citizens and Australians maintain their free healthcare at home upon returning from an overseas trip.

Don't forget to stock up on all of your regularly required prescription medications before traveling. It's possible that you can find the same products abroad, but if you can't, it's better not to find out the hard way. Ask your doctor and insurance provider how to best go about this depending on the coverage plan or condition being treated.

Travel Insurance

As for healthcare coverage abroad, a lot will depend on where you are and what the regulations are in each country. If you plan on being an expat, then check into the regulations in the country you plan to live in. If teaching, ask your placement agency about health insurance.

For those in a state of movement, the best option for healthcare coverage is travel insurance. In most cases, you will pay out of pocket and then get reimbursed for the expenses you incur on your travels, provided you demonstrate proof of care given. This usually means you must retain receipts, and some companies will ask that the healthcare provider fill out specific paperwork during your visit. Typically you have up to a year after the incident or doctor's visit to file a claim. Buying more months of coverage up front makes it cheaper overall.

Travel insurance can help you get to the help you need when things get serious. It's scary to think about, but it's a lot less scary to get sick and have coverage than to get sick and stuck with a huge hospital bill, or to get treated in a place where you're not confident in the level of care. (Would you rather have a medical emergency handled in developing Cambodia or in more medically advanced Singapore?) Even if you're traveling in countries where medical care is cheap, travel insurance can cover you if you need to be airlifted or require hospitalization or surgery. Insurance can even pay for a family member to come to you if you're immobile.

What questions should you ask when selecting a plan?

- Does it cover the activities I want to participate in?
- What kind of documentation do I have to provide if I have an incident?
- Does coverage extend to my electronics, or do I need a separate plan?
- Does it include trip-cancellation insurance?
- What happens if my baggage gets lost?
- Will I be covered if I return home with an illness?
- Does it include high-cost items like repatriation, airlifting, long hospital stays, and emergency evacuation?

I did quite a bit of research and read a lot of Internet forums before electing to go with World Nomads' Adventurer plan for my travels. Sure, many of the countries I visit are pretty cheap, and routine healthcare would not be too costly, but I also do a lot of scuba diving and trekking, and I drive rental cars from time to time. These riskier activities up my chances of having a problem. Small out-of-pocket doctor's visits are fine, but bigger and more expensive problems could arise. This particular plan covers a lot of sports, so for me, it makes sense and has been my go-to for the past five years of my travels.

For lifestyle changes and longer-term expat insurance, take a look at IM Global, which has options for families and offers coverage within the US, provided that you're out of the country for at least half the year.

For those over 70, Insure My Trip offers comprehensive packages.

Additionally, look into insurance provided by travel credit cards. Even if your travel insurance doesn't cover baggage loss or car rental issues, your credit card might at no additional cost.

Note: Many travel insurance companies exclude coverage in the United States (both for US citizens and visitors), so if your travels will be taking you there, make sure that your travel insurance includes such coverage. Medical bills in the United States are huge, so don't get stuck with one!

Packing: What's Really Essential?

The most important things to remember when packing are to bring what is comfortable and what is essential — then cut that in half and only bring what you can realistically carry.

Packing lists often suggest taking sweat-wicking fabrics, safari pants, and all kinds of other "practical" clothing. In theory this sounds smart, but in practice, most people want to still look good when traveling, and what makes sense to wear at home tends to make sense abroad as well, taking into account modesty requirements and climate in certain areas.

At first, I was kitted out in REI's finest and dorkiest-looking ensembles. I had the moisture-wicking clothing and the smart pants. Three months into my trip, when I mailed a box home with some gifts for my family, I also sent back my safari pants (come on, they're really not cute) and yoga pants (super thick yoga pants in Southeast Asian heat? What was I thinking?), and I only kept one moisture-wicking shirt for trekking.

A former nurse and solo traveler of six years, Rachel Jones, who wrote Hippie in Heels, agreed, saying,

On my first backpacking trip, I packed like a "backpacker" is told to. Now, six years later, I pack the same clothes that I use when I am at home, and the same shoes and toiletries. I always pack my favorite layering pieces, like a baggy crocheted kimono, leggings, perfect-fitting jeans shorts, a button-up linen shirt that I can tie around my waist, and a couple sarongs.

Packing lists

Ask yourself what you really, truly need. Gather together the items you think you'll want to take, and then get rid of half of them — seriously! The more you have to look after and the more weight you carry, the tougher it is to travel cheaply and easily, since you'll often have to pay for checked baggage and taxis. It's also much tougher to keep all of your belongings in sight when there's a lot of them, and to walk any sort of distance — if your belongings are always with you, theft is much less likely, and walking around to find accommodations or to get from point A to point B will be much less painful.

Does that mean doing without variety? Not really, because by only bringing along clothing that isn't super expensive and leaving room in your bag for purchases, you can ditch, donate, or trade clothes with a fellow traveler or buy new things if you get tired of that shirt or if those shorts get a hole in them.

In Indonesia, sitting next to the carry-on–sized bag I had used for the previous ten months

The following are some sample packing lists, along with suggestions for clothing, electronics, and other essentials:

Clothing

Hot and dry climates:

- 4–6 light tank tops

- 1–2 short-sleeved shirts

- 1–2 lightweight dresses or skirts, particularly in places where modesty is a consideration

- 3–4 pairs of shorts, both for exercise and fashion

- Enough undies for at least a week

- 2–3 pairs of ankle socks

- 1 pair of flip-flops or sandals

- 1 pair of running shoes

- Hat for shade in the sun

- 1 lightweight shawl to cover up if needed

- 1–2 pairs of warm leggings for nights

- Warm jacket for nights

- Light gloves and beanie for nights

- Cute sunglasses

Hot and humid climates:

- 4–6 light tank tops (if in Southeast Asia, leave room to buy some there)

- 1–2 short-sleeved shirts

- 2 pairs of harem pants

- 1 lightweight dress or skirt, particularly in places where modesty is a consideration

- 1 pair of lightweight trekking pants (if entering the jungle)

- 2 pairs of shorts, both for exercise and fashion (not denim — it sucks in humidity)

- Enough undies for at least a week

- 2–3 pairs of ankle socks

- 1 pair of flip-flops or sandals

- 1 pair of running shoes

- 1 very lightweight jacket

- Hat for shade in the sun

- 1 sarong to cover up if needed and for the beach

- 2 swimsuits

- Cute sunglasses

Temperate climates:

- 3–4 tank tops, crops, or a mix

- 2–3 pairs of patterned leggings (I usually take fashionable and workout leggings)

- 1–2 thin long-sleeved shirts for layering

- 2 lightweight dresses, overalls, and/or rompers

- 1–2 pairs of pants (I think pants are leg prison so I bring more leggings)

- Enough undies for at least a week

- 2–3 pairs of ankle socks

- 1 pair of sandals or flip-flops

- 1 pair of boots

- 1 pair of running shoes

- 1–2 jackets (fashionable and for activities)

- 2 swimsuits

- Cute sunglasses

Cold climates

- 4–5 thin shirts for layering

- 2 thermal shirts

- 1–2 sweaters

- 2 pairs of fleece-lined leggings

- 2 pairs of normal leggings

- 1 pair of loose jeans that you can fit leggings underneath

- Enough undies for at least a week

- 4–5 pairs of thick socks

- 1 bathing suit for those snowy hot tubs

- 1 very warm winter jacket

- 2 pairs snow boots

- 1 pair gloves and hat

The above lists intentionally leave room for purchases on the road. Buying clothing abroad usually makes sense: it is suited to the environment weather-wise and in terms of style, is often cheaper than clothing back home, and is a nice and functional souvenir to bring home with you.

Laundry is easy to do on the road and pretty cheap in many parts of the world. When laundry services aren't available, handwashing in the hotel room sink and hanging on a portable line is an option, as is taking advantage of a washing machine at your guesthouse or apartment rental.

Toiletries

- 4 refillable 100ml bottles for shampoo, face wash, body wash, and conditioner

- 1 small lotion bottle, under 100ml

- 1 facial moisturizer bottle (under 100ml) for each three months of the trip

- A small first aid kit: spray Neosporin, 20 Band-Aids, OTC painkillers (such as paracetamol/ acetaminophen), gauze, medical tape, anti-itch cream and/or pills, antidiarrheals

- 1 tube of sunscreen, under 100ml

- 1 small bug spray bottle, if needed

- 1–2 nonspray deodorants (can be purchased abroad)

- 1 razor and enough refills for the trip (one razor per two months)

- 1 packet of hair ties, elastic headband, and bobby pins

- Nail clippers

- Tweezers

- 1 eyeglasses repair kit

- 1 small toiletry bag for organization

- 1 towel

If the above amounts seem small, remember that toiletries and over-the-counter painkillers can be refilled and replaced on the road. Pantene shampoo seems to be universal, as does soap, face wash, lotions, sunscreen, and conditioner. Ladies abroad use these things, too.

Makeup

- 1–2 palettes of eye shadow (smoky and neutrals)

- 1 light powder foundation and bronzer

- 2–3 application brushes

- 1–2 eyeliner and mascara bottles

It's best to leave the straighteners and dryers at home and embrace your natural hair. I never once saw a traveler in Southeast Asia styling her hair — it would just blow a fuse.

Note: Makeup-wise, in developing countries it's rare that travelers wear any, but when they do, it's usually just some eyeliner and mascara, which are small and pack easily.

Diva Cup

Now onto the girly stuff: that monthly visitor we all love so much doesn't stop visiting while on the road. Tampons are available in most countries you might wish to visit, but in some they are nowhere to be found. In China, for example, I could only find sanitary napkins, which I haven't dealt with since middle school. No thank you.

Enter the Diva Cup, a silicone cup insert that comes in pre- and post-childbirth sizes and can be cleaned and reused. (The water that you wash your body with is also fine to wash the Diva Cup with. There's also DivaWash, which you can bring along if you'd like something other than soap.) The Diva Cup actually saves a lot of money in the long run, is more environmentally friendly, and best of all, can be worn for up to 12 hours at a time (just be sure

to follow the directions to avoid any leakage). It's a life —
or rather week — saver. All hail the Diva Cup!

Birth control can be purchased abroad but with limited
brand availability and varying refill requirements. It's best
to prepare by bringing enough along with you. Condoms
can be purchased on the road at just about any
convenience store.

Computer

- *The* 13-inch MacBook Air *is a great compact and light
  option. It's not powerful enough for video editing
  software and could have more storage space, but it
  works for most digital nomad needs.*

- Netbooks *are a cheap alternative to computers if you
  mostly want a computer to stay in touch and surf the
  web.*

- Not doing much typing? Tablets are a great
  lightweight and cheaper option for staying in touch,
  uploading photos, and using apps.

Cameras and photography

The photography equipment listed here is what I travel
with as a photography enthusiast. It's a bit pricey, so if it's
out of your range, consider taking photos with a
smartphone or reasonably priced point-and-shoot. Or
consider buying a used camera from a reputable local
reseller, where you can see and test the camera prior to
purchasing.

- The Sony a6000 is an excellent starter mirrorless digital camera. What does this mean? A mirrorless camera is typically lighter weight than a DSLR (digital single-lens reflex) camera. Both typically have a higher pixel level and more settings than a point-and-shoot, plus you can change the lenses depending on your needs. The photos are much better as a result, and on the trip of a lifetime, you want awesome photos, right?

- An additional zoom lens for wildlife photography and portraiture

- A Pacsafe camera strap is generic looking and very difficult to cut.

- Consider a GoPro for underwater or sporting videos and photos. If you're not ready to commit to a mirrorless, use a GoPro instead. Get extra batteries and a charger, as the battery life on GoPros is quite short.

- A portable charger for smartphones and cameras

- Traveling solo means taking selfies from time to time. Embrace the selfie stick!

- Lightroom is a user-friendly program that can be a game changer, the difference between photos that are just OK and photos that are fantastic.

- A portable hard drive for backups when the Internet connection is too weak to upload to a cloud server

If you're new to photography and want some help learning the ropes, YouTube can be a great resource. Just type in your camera model and "tutorial" and see what it comes back with. If you want to elevate to a more professional level, consider a course that gives you access to a successful pro, like Laurence Norah's course.

Gear

Backpack

I travel with a backpack because I find it to be much more convenient than suitcases in most of the world. In Europe, dragging small wheels over cobblestone streets can get pretty annoying, and in much of the developing world, there aren't any sidewalks to speak of, or they're cracked and full of dirt. Backpacks allow easy navigation of stairs and uneven pavement.

How should you pick the right backpack? Consider the following:

- **Try it on in person with weight in it:** Walk around the store for at least ten minutes with each pack on to determine which is the most comfortable for your body.

- **Make sure it fits:** A great backpack should fit snugly around your body, with the waist straps providing ample weight distribution.

- **Front Load vs. Top load:** Front-load packs are easier to work with and more suitcase-like than a top-load bag, which can be pretty annoying if the one thing you need is at the bottom of the bag

- **Extra compartments:** A backpack with a few side and top compartments is helpful for organization

- **Cover it:** Make sure that it comes with a rain cover.

In the United States, REI is a great store, with a dedicated team in the backpacking department to help make suggestions. I've used my REI Vagabond Tour 40 Travel Pack for two years now and nothing on it has broken, which is impressive given how much I pack it to the brim and the constant use it gets.

Packing cubes

If there's one absolutely essential item to packing light it's the packing cube. They help tremendously with organization, keeping dirty and clean clothes separate, and saving space by compressing clothing with the zipper sides. Combat wrinkles by rolling and stacking clothing items next to each other in the cube. It works like a charm. One cube fits perfectly into a 35–40-liter backpack, allowing you to pack more clothing than otherwise possible by organizing and compacting it in a zipped-up packing cube.

Thief-safe travel gear

- Use a Pacsafe messenger bag as a day bag, especially for towns like Phnom Penh or Ho Chi Minh City, where drive-by motorbike thieves and bag-slashers are a constant threat. There is a wire running through the strap, the colors are not flashy, and it is equipped with hidden pockets that block RFID readers from scanning passport and credit card information.

- If carrying large cameras, the Camsafe Carrying Case for Cameras, which slings over one shoulder and fits close to the body; it's great for trekking and is the perfect carrier for cameras, passport, Kindle, and wallet.

- The Pacsafe backpack and bag protector is a wire mesh bag that protects valuables if you're in a place without lockers or a safe and aren't actively using the bag. Whether in dorms, private rooms, bamboo bungalows, the trunk of a rental car, or wooden huts, it is a huge contributor to peace of mind and takes up very little space. Slip on the bag's rain jacket, wrap the bag in the Pacsafe bag protector, then use an additional lock to secure it to a bunk bed bedpost or any other object in the room that is fixed to the floor or wall and would be difficult to remove.

Leave behind mosquito nets, pillows, and sleeping bags. In the case that any of these are needed, there will usually an easy way to obtain them, whether by borrowing, renting, or buying for cheap on the road.

Hopefully these tips from the past five years of my travels — having learned a bit here and there — will help you to pack a bit lighter and more confidently. Remember, less is more!

Banking

Selecting the right bank and cash withdrawal method is a pretty essential part to keeping as much of your savings as possible for your trip, and making sure that you can access it while traveling

Many bank accounts have high fees, especially for international withdrawals, and don't offer much in the way of benefits. Look at your monthly statements, or call the bank, and see if fees are charged each month, whether the interest is high or low, and what the penalties are for international withdrawals.

Charles Schwab in the United States refunds all ATM fees and does not charge foreign transaction fees. Yes, you do have to open a brokerage account with them to access the bank account, but you don't have to actively use the brokerage account. I save at least $50 per month in refunded ATM fees. This is my main bank, and I recommend it to everyone traveling abroad.

Other banks that offer savings accounts with no fees and high interest are Discover Bank, Virtual Bank, and Capital One 360. If none of the above are an option in your country, take a look at banks that are part of the Global ATM Alliance, a group of international banks that have agreed not to assess international ATM access fees to customers of member banks. Fewer fees help tremendously to preserve your money abroad.

Here's a listing of banks in this network:

- ABSA (South Africa)

- Banca Nazionale del Lavoro (Italy)

- Bank of America (United States)

- Barclays (England, Wales, Spain, Portugal, Gibraltar, and certain countries in Africa)

- BNP Paribas (France, Ukraine)

- China Construction Bank (China; Bank of America cardholders only)

- Deutsche Bank (Germany, Poland, Czech Republic, Spain, Portugal, and Italy)

- Santander Serfin (Mexico; Bank of America cardholders only)

- Scotiabank (Canada, Caribbean, Peru, Chile, and Mexico)

- UkrSibbank (Ukraine)

- Westpac (Australia, New Zealand, Fiji, Vanuatu, Cook Islands, Samoa, Tonga, Papua New Guinea, and Solomon Islands)

Don't stress if your card doesn't have a chip and a PIN number. Having cards with this function does make purchases and banking quicker in Europe, Australia, and South Africa, but you can still use a card with a magnetic strip to buy things and withdraw cash. I have never encountered a situation where only cards with chips were accepted.

For non-US citizens, I like these two cards:

- Citibank Australia

- Norwich & Peterborough Building Society (UK residents)

Have a backup

For emergency's sake, have a backup ATM card and bank account with a bit of cash in it that charges low or no fees. If the ATM machine eats your card, your bank puts a hold on your card, or your card is stolen, you'll have a backup method to get cash in emergency situations. By having a backup, there's no need to trouble anyone at home to wire over money; besides, Western Union is expensive. It's also good to have one MasterCard and one Visa, as some ATMs will only take one or the other.

For additional backup, always be sure to have crisp US dollars available in denominations over $20. It is the easiest currency to exchange if you can't find an ATM, and many borders, such as Tanzania, Vietnam, and Cambodia, will charge way higher visa rates if paid in anything other than US dollars (including the local currency).

I learned this the hard way when, after an ATM didn't give my card back and for whatever reason I failed to notice, I suddenly found myself with the equivalent of only about $30 while standing in front of another ATM in Thailand a week later, frantically looking for my (missing) debit card. It was nowhere to be found, and I didn't have any US dollars on me to change at a moneychanger. I had made two rookie mistakes simultaneously.

Thankfully a fellow traveler sympathized with my situation and was able to give me some cash, but if I had had a backup card, it wouldn't have mattered and I could have saved myself the stress.

It also helps if you can add a trustworthy person to your one of your accounts. I added my mother, so that if any checks come through or something pops up at a time and place where I'd have trouble handling it, she can sort it out. When I was in Botswana without access to a phone line and my bank called her to report suspicious spending, she checked my Twitter, saw where I was, and had the authority to call back and ask them to remove the hold on my card. If there's someone you can really trust with that kind of access, it's a good idea.

Getting local currency

If using ATMs with a card with low or no fees, such as Charles Schwab, there's no need to carry large sums of cash or to use moneychangers, who are in the business of making a profit and will never give you the best exchange rate.

If using ATMs that are part of the Global ATM Alliance, look for those in major cities and consider getting your cash before heading to smaller towns that may not have as many options available.

To avoid bad exchange rates and ATMs that may have been tampered with, it's best to use ATMs that are inside of or connected to a bank. Some ATMs have been fitted by thieves with illegal card-reading technology designed to steal your info, but you can be sure that an ATM inside of a bank will be safe. Plus, standalone ATMs and those inside of a convenience store are more likely to charge high fees and offer poor exchange rates.

If you must use a moneychanger, smartphone apps such *GlobeConvert Free* allow you to view the most recent exchange rates so that you can make more informed purchasing and changing decisions. Avoid the airport or unlicensed changers standing at land borders. They will give you the worst exchange rate, since they're banking on the fact that you've just arrived and might not yet know the proper exchange rate.

Every time you use your card overseas, your local bank coverts the transaction into your local currency for billing purposes and takes a little off the top for doing so. Thus the official rate you see online is not what you actually get. That's the interbank rate, and unless you become a major bank, you're not going to get that rate. All we can do is get as close as we can to that rate. To avoid being on the real losing end of conversion, follow the following tips:

- Use a credit card: Credit card companies get the best rates. Using a credit card will get you an exchange rate closest to the official interbank currency rate so avoid an ATM or cash if you can.

- **Use an ATM:** ATMs offer the best exchange rate after credit cards. They aren't as good as credit cards since commercial banks take a little more off the top, but it's much better than exchanging cash.

- **Don't use money exchangers:** Money exchange offices offer the worst rates because they are so far down the food chain, they can't get the best exchange rate (plus, they usually charge a commission as well). Another tip: avoid using the company Travelex at all costs — they have worst rates and fees. Never, never use them. Avoid their ATMs too!

- **Don't change money at airports:** The rates you see at airports are the worst — never, ever use an exchange bureau there unless you absolutely have to.

- **Don't use ATMs in weird locations:** Using those ATMs you find in hotels, hostels, local 7-11s, or some other random place is a bad idea. They're convenient, but you'll pay for that convenience. They always charge high ATM fees and offer horrible conversion rates. Skip those ATMs and find a major bank.

- **Always pick the local currency:** When you use your credit card abroad, you will often be given the option to be charged in your home currency (i.e., instead of being charged in euros, they will charge you in US dollars). Never say yes. The rate at which they are converting the currency is always worse than the rate your bank will give you. Pick the local currency and let your credit card company make the conversion. You'll get a better rate.

Travel credit cards

Travel credit cards are a great way to build up mileage credit and to carry around less cash. When possible, I charge everything I would normally buy — from my groceries to a pack of gum — at the gas station instead of using cash, just to build up mileage points. I pay off my card in full each month, never overspending, since that would defeat the purpose of the perks.

Travel credit cards offer a great opportunity to earn free points that can be redeemed for airfares, hotels, or cold hard cash. In the race to get customers, credit card–issuing companies partner with various travel brands (or just simply offer their own card) to entice consumers with sign-up bonuses, loyalty points, special discounts, and more. Their desire to get you, the consumer, is really your gain. By milking the system, you can get tons of free air tickets, hotel rooms, vacations, and even cash back.

What to look for in a travel rewards card:

A huge sign-up bonus: A big sign-up bonus (after you meet the minimum spending requirement) is what jump-starts your mileage account and gets you close to a free flight (sometimes these bonuses even get you a few free flights!). Don't sign up for a card unless it offers a high sign-up bonus.

Bonuses work like this: in order to get the large bonuses, you must make either a single purchase or meet a minimum spending threshold in a certain time frame. After that, depending on the card, you can earn 1–5x points per dollar spent.

- Starwood or Platinum Card from American Express (airline rebates, Uber credits)

- Chase Sapphire Preferred or Reserve (generous sign-up bonus and points)

- American Express Premier Rewards Gold Card (3x points on flights)

- Chase Ink Bold (for businesses)

- Citi Prestige (for the perks)

- Lufthansa Miles & More (For Germans)

- American Express Explorer Card (For Australians)

- Air New Zealand cards (For Kiwis)

Added category spending bonus: Most credit cards offer one point for every dollar spent. However, the good credit cards will give you extra points when you shop at specific retailers, or, if it is a branded credit card, with a particular brand. This will help you earn points much more quickly. For example, with the Chase Sapphire Preferred card you get 2x points for travel and dining at restaurants, the Chase Ink gives you 5x points for office spending, and the American Express Premier Rewards Gold card gives 3x points on airfare. I try to get and use cards in my day-to-day spending that give me more than just one mile per dollar spent.

Low spending minimum: Unfortunately, in order to get the great bonuses these cards offer, there is usually a required spending minimum. While there are ways to fake your spending, it's best to be able to get the bonus using normal day-to-day spending. I typically sign up for cards with a minimum spending requirement of $1,000–3,000

USD in a three- to six-month period. My favorite spending minimums are the offers that require you to make one purchase in order to unlock the bonus!

Managing your ability to meet the minimum spending requirements is key because if you are spending more money than you usually do just to get these points, the points are no longer free. Only spend what you normally would and not a penny more.

It's easy to go crazy and sign up for 10 cards in a short amount of time. But then to get the bonus points, you might find yourself stuck with having to spend $10,000–30,000 USD in a very short period of time. That's a lot of pressure. While you shouldn't necessarily avoid high-minimum-spending cards as they have substantial rewards, it's a good idea to start small because you don't want to get stuck with so many cards that you can't meet the minimum spends.

Also, once you get a card, you can't reapply for the card, so don't go overboard and miss out on the sign-up bonus.

That's why having a goal and starting small is important with credit cards. You don't want to dive into the deep end before you're ready, because one mistake in this game can leave you stuck with spending requirements you can't meet (and bonus points you can't earn)!

Special perks: All of these travel credit cards offer great perks. Many will give you special elite loyalty status or other extra perks. I want cards without foreign transaction fees and with free checked baggage, priority boarding, free nights, etc. It's not just about just getting miles; it's about what else comes with the card that makes my life easier!

Annual fees: No one likes paying annual fees for credit cards. Many of the fees for company branded credit cards range from $50 to $95 per year. I pay an annual fee. For those who travel a lot and fly a lot, I think it is worth it to get a card with a fee. Fee-based cards tend to give you a better rewards scheme, where you can accumulate points faster, get better access to services and special offers, and get better travel protection. With these cards, I have saved more money on travel than I have spent on fees.

Foreign transaction fees: The majority of credit cards charge a 3% fee when you use them overseas. Credit cards are great to use because you get a good exchange rate from them, but if you are paying a fee every time you use the card, then it become less good. The simplest card for avoiding foreign fees is the Capital One Venture Card. There is no yearly fee but there's also no rewards structure (OK, there is but it sucks — here's why). This card is for people who want simplicity and don't care about points (though that's just crazy talk).

However, if you decide you do want points and see the value in the yearly fee (which is usually pretty low, see above), the best cards for avoiding overseas fees are the Chase Sapphire Preferred, Starwood American Express, Barclay's Arrival Plus, Chase Ink, or any airline branded card. They are way better than the Capital One card, but everyone's spending needs are different, right?!

Which credit card should you get?

With so many credit cards to choose from, which ones do you pick? Well, the short answer is: all of them. Grab as many as you can. Why put a limit on how many points you can get?

But that being said, when you are just beginning to learn this stuff, you should start off with the following question:

What is your goal?

Are you interested in loyalty to a brand, free rewards, or avoiding fees? Do you want to milk the rewards and bonus system to get free flights, or do you just want a card that won't charge you a fee for using it at that restaurant in Brazil? Is elite status the most important perk for you? Just want free hotel rooms?

For example, if you're a loyal flier with American Airlines, the best cards to start off with would be the Citi American AAdvantage card (50,000 point sign-up bonus) and the Starwood American Express card (25,000 sign-up bonus plus 20% transfer bonus that you can use with your AA account).

If you just want points to spend wherever you choose, get the Chase or American Express cards because you can use their points with a variety of travel companies. They each have their own rewards programs (Chase Ultimate Rewards and American Express Membership Rewards), and points can be transferred to multiple airline or hotel partners and used to book travel directly through their sites.

By first focusing on what you want, you can maximize your short-term goals and get the hang of travel hacking. For example, I tend to avoid hotel cards since I rarely stay in hotels. I dislike Hilton and Marriott and would rather focus on getting points related to Starwood (I prefer their hotels) or miles for flying. So unless there is an excellent sign-up bonus for a certain card, I concentrate my efforts on what matters most to me: using cards that get me airline miles or that have good transfer bonuses to airline programs.

Check out *Frequent Miler* and *The Points Guy* for the most up-to-date information on the best rewards currently available. If you want to take it a step further and are interested in travel hacking — a method for racking up hotel and mileage credits using creative collection methods — take a look at Matt Kepnes's *Ultimate Guide to Travel Hacking*.

Note: Keep in mind that in some countries, such as most developing nations, using credit cards isn't possible and cash is king. If you plan on spending a particularly long time in these countries without much of a chance to build up reward points, consider whether if you can spend enough with the card before you go or after the trip to justify the annual fee.

Mail

Hopefully most of your bills have been scrapped, since you will presumably no longer have rent and utility payments. If you have an outstanding student loan or other payments, try to make them all paperless, i.e., payable online or even automated.

For any additional mail that comes in, I usually kindly ask my mother to keep it for me and inform me of anything pressing.

If your mail can't be sent to a (very understanding) family member, consider a P.O. box for only the most important senders, or alert your mail service that you'll be gone and need them to hold your mail.

Phone Contracts

If you are under contract with your phone plan, call and see if they offer a "disabled" or "maintenance" mode. In the United States, my former carrier, AT&T, was able to do this for six months for $10/month. It wasn't ideal pay $10 for absolutely nothing, but the alternative was $75 per month for absolutely nothing. Verizon offers something similar, as do Canada's largest carrier, Rogers and O2 in the UK.

Buying a local SIM and having connectivity has helped me out of a sticky situation on more than one occasion.

Some plans are international, such as T-Mobile's and O2's, but most are not. In the case that your plan is not, using it abroad will be costly. Keep your phone's data roaming turned off and only use it to surf the web when there's Wi-Fi.

I find that the best method is to travel around with an unlocked smartphone and to buy local SIM cards on the ground. That means that instead of signing a contract with your provider in order to get a discount on a phone purchase, you pay full price to get a phone that isn't tied to any one network. It means more money up front, but I find that it saves me big-time in the long run. If that's too much of a cash outlay, consider buying a used phone instead.

In most countries, local SIM cards are cheaper than the international plans offered by T-Mobile and O2 if you plan on staying for a while and especially if you are in the developing world, where data is cheap. (In Vietnam, for example, three gigabytes' worth of 4G data costs less than $10.) They also offer better data connectivity than a shared Wi-Fi connection in a hostel or hotel.

International plans can be more helpful if you're moving around quickly, such as a European trip that covers several countries in a short amount of time. However, many European providers do cover the entire continent, such as Vodafone, while T-Mobile might not cover every country you plan on visiting. Personally, I'd buy local.

Buying a local SIM and having connectivity has helped me out of a sticky situation on more than one occasion. I've been able to make calls to hostels when I was stranded, could quickly book a guesthouse while riding in the back of a tuk-tuk, and best of all, had a GPS with me in the form of Google Maps.

Bring along a passport when buying a SIM card, as some stores will require it to process the application. Make sure that the data is working before you walk out of the store, in case there are extra steps you need to take in order to activate it. Always go with prepaid cards that can be refilled on a monthly basis.

If you've done all of the aforementioned and bought your gear, congratulations! You've gotten through the toughest part of planning your trip and deserve a pat on the back. (Nobody around to do that? Give yourself a pat on the back. Grab both shoulders and squeeze.) Give yourself a self-high five. The hard part is done. Now all that's left to do is go.

In the following chapters we'll look into the things you can do to stay safe and connected once you're already on the road, and to have the best time possible. The best is yet to come!

Staying Safe and Connected:
Ignore Rumors and Dare Greatly

Reaching goals isn't for pessimistic people. At all steps of my [life], there was someone saying, "I wouldn't do that. You're too old, too young, too inexperienced." There are always naysayers. Ask yourself: What is important to me?

—FRANCE CÓRDOVA, the youngest and first female NASA Chief Scientist

One of the chief concerns for most would-be solo travelers is safety. For many women, it's the biggest barrier to traveling alone. Why have we barely touched on it until now? Because in reality, staying safe is easy. You already have the skills you need: the same methods you use to stay safe at home.

Would you walk around alone at night back at home? Would you take your phone out in certain parts of the city or neighborhoods that are known for theft? Would you go out by yourself and get intoxicated at a bar where you knew no one? If you said "no" to all of these scenarios, then chances are the skills you already have are more than enough to keep you safe on the road.

Women fear that traveling solo makes them a target. However, traveling solo allows you to be hyperaware of your surroundings. If nobody is there to distract you, it's easier to notice little things, to take note of street signs, and to not get lost as easily. Plus, over time your intuition becomes sharper.

There's much to be said about the power of intuition. If something or someone gives you an uneasy vibe, there's no shame in walking away or saying no. If your gut is telling you that something doesn't feel right, listen to it. This sense naturally becomes more heightened over time as a solo traveler. It's surprising how much listening to that little voice in the back of your mind can steer you in the right direction.

Manouk, a solo female traveler and doctor from the Netherlands, adds,

You will soon notice you learn to trust your instincts. Is this person trustworthy or not? Is it safe to go out now? Make sure you're prepared for "emergency situations"; make friends (even during a short bus ride); be friendly, polite, and patient; and always act confident. Make sure you have the right mind-set (easy-going and open-minded), and solo traveling is truly a piece of cake!

How to Avoid Being a Target: Tips and Tricks

The following are some tried-and-true techniques picked up from five years of solo travels, and from speaking to others about what has worked for them:

Know when to say "no"

Don't compromise your comfort levels by only saying "yes" when it feels right to say "no." Sometimes in bars and hostels, the group mentality to keep drinking and the pressure to partake in yet another round of shots is present on a daily basis. Getting too intoxicated is dangerous, and saying no feels good sometimes.

Don't be afraid to disappoint people if you need to decline a night out. You earn your own self-respect that way, and nothing is more important than that. It's OK to imbibe sometimes, but pace yourself. Your solo journey is about your enjoyment and nobody else's.

Talk to locals

Ask them what you need to be aware of and which local scams and areas of town to avoid. When I was in Ho Chi Minh City, for example, the super helpful staff at my hostel told me to be careful with my cell phone out on the streets and to beware of bag-snatching thieves. Given this, when I went out at night I only took a bit of money in a pocket in my shorts that buttoned, and I left everything else in the hostel locker, and my room key at the reception desk.

Blend in

One of the easiest ways to stay safe is to blend in as much as possible and to do as the locals do. Of course, in many countries you visit, it will be clear that you are most definitely a tourist. However the less flashy you are and the more you dress in the local style and learn respectful hand gestures and how to address people, the better.

Learning a few local words endears you to those who live there, as well. Speaking a few words — most importantly, greetings and thank-yous — has a big impact on how you're perceived.

Dress appropriately and understand local customs

It's a sad truth that women don't have the same rights as men in much of the world. Chances are good that there are places in this world where you will have to accept the fact that as a female, you cannot act as you please and the law will treat you differently based on sex.

For example, over 50 countries observe sharia law to varying degrees, which means that Islamic guidelines are followed in some form or another. In these places, respecting the local law and people usually means considering what you're wearing; usually it's best to at least cover your shoulders and knees. The extent to which it's important to cover more than that — and how women's rights might differ from men's — depends on the country. This does not mean, however, that all countries that practice sharia law will result in the need to cover up, nor does it mean that women need only cover up in countries that practice sharia law.

It's important for each female traveler to research local modesty laws and customs prior to visiting any given country. The World Economic Forum's 2016 Gender Gap Report has profiled most countries and is a helpful guide for women's rights and expectations abroad. *Journeywoman* has suggestions for what to wear in just about every country as well.

Carry a dummy wallet

In order to keep the most important valuables safe, use a dummy wallet, which contains some canceled credit cards and just a little bit of cash. It's enough to make thieves think they are getting something worthwhile in the unfortunate event that you do get robbed.

Most thieves want a quick getaway, so handing over your cheap bag or dummy wallet lets them get away with something tangible, but the good stuff will still be with you. There will be no struggle or hesitation, and you can remain safe.

This isn't necessary in most Asian countries, but in South Africa and South and Central America, where muggings are quite common, it may be a precaution worth taking.

Also, stick your phone in your bra, roll up most of your money and put it in your shoe, and keep keys in your front pocket.

Find a way to make noise

Another important tool is something that makes noise. A whistle can come in handy if you're ever lost, need to scare off rabid monkeys (it works!), or find yourself in some other situation where alerting those around you to your distress would be helpful. You never know how useful something so small can be.

I once received a comment from a reader who suggested carrying a portable door alarm as well, citing a time when a hostel owner had tried to open her door while she was sleeping. This seems like a great asset to have along for peace of mind, especially considering how cheap they are.

Another commenter on the same post wrote, "Stay in a room close to the elevators, not at the end of a hall, where criminals go for the privacy. Never stay on the ground floor, especially if there's a door to the outside or windows. Another traveler I knew carried a door jamb with her."

It might not be possible to stay high up during your travels — bamboo bungalows don't come in two stories — but if you're in a city with that option, aim high.

Keep your head up and walk with confidence

There's a lot to be said about being the least attractive target. When I'm traveling alone, I look people in the eye, I'm assertive, and I walk with confidence. I give off the vibe that I'm not going to take any crap from anyone, and if someone messes with me, I certainly won't take it quietly.

Walk the walk, and communicate with your body language that you're not to be messed with. This goes a long way!

Stay alert and look around

When I'm walking on the sidewalk, I make sure that I'm always looking around and that I'm not distracted by my phone or headphones. If someone comes up behind me, I'll hear it. If someone is walking near me, I make sure that he/she knows and that I've acknowledged them.

If you ever feel threatened, walk closer to another group, particularly a family or local women who would see someone mugging you, or duck into a store until the perceived threat has passed.

Do not walk alone at night

Men and women alike are most likely to become targets at night. It's dark, people are unlikely to see the altercation, and when you're alone, you're easy to overpower.

If you must go out at night, pay up for a taxi, or ask someone at your hostel if they'd like to come with you. The only time I've had an issue is when I broke my own rule and went out alone after dark. Learn from my mistakes and bring someone with you if you must go out after the sun goes down.

Do not get too intoxicated

You wouldn't go out and get drunk alone at a bar at home, right? Don't do it on the road, either! Keep your drinking to a minimum, and if that's hard to do, have a sober trip.

The benefits are twofold: You stay safe, and you get to save more money and spend less time hungover during your trip!

Should you carry pepper spray?

Pepper spray key chains can work for car or train travel but for air travel, if you plan to pack carry-on only, pepper spray is a no-no (as are knives). In checked baggage it is sometimes confiscated as well, although according to TSA guidelines, it is allowed if it has a safety mechanism.

Pepper spray is also illegal in many countries and/or treated as a concealed weapon, even if you're arriving by car or train. Mosquito repellant, as an alternative, causes a similar burning sensation in the eyes and is allowed on airplanes.

Sometimes, it's best to lie

You'll often be asked where your boyfriend or husband is. Honesty isn't always the best policy. Feel out the situation to discern if it's just a friendly question. If it's a friendly female asking, she is probably a bit shocked to see a woman out traveling on her own — it might not be common in her culture.

Most of the time, however, if someone asks within the first two questions of a conversation or if it's a male driver or someone on the street, you should say you're on your way to meet your boyfriend. There's no shame in lying if it's self-preservation — and it's none of his business anyway.

Read up on dangers and annoyances before you go

In addition, before you visit a country, research common scams and dangers and keep up with the current political climate of your destination on a travel information website. For Americans, that would be the *Bureau of Consular Affairs*, for Canadians it's *Travel Advice and Advisories*, in the UK it's *Foreign Travel Advice*, and in Australia it's *Smartraveller*. These websites all more or less give the same information.

While it's important to make sure you're familiar with threats and dangers, don't take it to mean that everything will be scary, and keep in mind that these sites may be taking a more extreme stance than is necessary.

When the coup d'état was announced in Thailand in May 2014, I was sitting in a sleepy beach town on the Thai island of Koh Chang, eating soup and laughing with friends. I'd always thought something like a military takeover would result in riots in the streets and the immediate evacuation of any foreigners in the country.

In this case it just meant that an earlier curfew would be enforced and otherwise — for tourists — everything was business as usual. There weren't explosions in the streets, there were no riots, and the same woman selling coconut shakes each morning was still there, offering up the cool and sweet drink.

The media abroad reported on the few-and–far-between clashes between the military and various political parties as though they were rampant. In reality I felt completely safe.

The same was true when I traveled to Mindanao in the Philippines, a region with frequent kidnappings and terrorist activity. While it's true that some parts of Mindanao experience such things, the island that I visited, Camiguin, had never experienced any of that negativity, and it had some of the friendliest people I met over the course of my month in the Philippines.

It's important to be aware, but don't let government warnings scare you away from taking your trip altogether.

How to Be Prepared If There's a Problem

Hopefully you won't ever encounter any issues while on your travels. However, just like back at home, things can and do go wrong from time to time. Here are a few ways to be prepared if it happens to you:

Know local emergency numbers

Don't have an unlocked smartphone? Buy a cheap phone just meant for calls and texts just in case there's an emergency.

Look up the local emergency number online before you land, or ask the staff at the front desk wherever you're staying. The best-case scenario is that you never have to use it, but it's always smart to be prepared just in case.

Know where the nearest hospital is

Every time you arrive in a new place, make sure you know where the nearest medical help is. If going to an area without great medical facilities, it's good to know this ahead of time in order to beef up the first aid kit and to rethink dangerous activities.

Have emergency cash

Stash cash in various parts of your luggage — ideally only the bags that stay with you in transit — just in case something gets stolen or a card gets lost. Keep this in cash rather than traveler's checks, which are a thing of the past and no longer used internationally. The best currency to have on hand is US dollars, as it is universally accepted at moneychangers. (Refer to the section above about dummy wallets as well for advice on how to keep your cash safe.)

Make copies of important documents

Prepare for the worst by carrying copies of all of your important travel documents, such as insurance forms, your passport, proof of immunizations, your driver's license, and proof of ownership of anything for which you might need to make a travel insurance claim. Keep a few hard copies, as well as electronic ones uploaded to a cloud server such as *Dropbox*.

Travel insurance companies tend to have strict rules on reimbursement, and that means they might ask for proof that you owned and used a stolen or lost item, and proof that it has been stolen. Take pictures of yourself holding each of the items, keep all associated receipts electronically and physically, and get a police report if anything is stolen. Ask your guesthouse or hotel concierge to help you do this if there are language or communication issues.

Know where the nearest consulate is

Look up where the nearest embassy, consulate, or diplomatic mission for your country is. In most cases, it will be in the capital city. A visit will be necessary should you lose your passport abroad, if you get arrested or have other legal trouble, or if there's a national emergency or natural disaster.

If visiting a country that your government has warnings for, it might be a good idea to register with your foreign affairs department or ministry and to let them know that you're going. In most cases this can be done online. Be sure to double-check that your travel insurance will cover you in these places, as sometimes coverage is revoked for areas known for high kidnapping rates and with government-issued warnings.

Stay Connected with Friends and Family

Another way to stay safe — and to help your family and friends worry less — is to stay connected.

I mentioned in the banking section that my mother knew where I was thanks to my Twitter feed. I keep a travel blog and update my Snapchat, Instagram, and Facebook regularly. Plus, I speak to my family and friends on a regular basis. It's fun to go off the grid from time to time, but still important to let your friends and family know where you are.

Wi-Fi is much more common in the world than it once was. It's easy to communicate for free with friends and family by using smartphone, computer, and tablet applications. The best is KakaoTalk, a South Korean app that allows free calls when both parties are using the app, routed through the country with the fastest Internet in the world. Even with a slow connection, Kakao can usually send a message through.

Facebook and WhatsApp now have a free voice and video calling tools as well. Those with Apple products can use FaceTime, anyone can use Google Hangouts, and Skype is an option in places with stronger Internet connections. Viber, LINE, and Tango are also free.

The information discussed in this chapter isn't meant to scare you or to turn you off from any parts of the world, but all of the aforementioned should be taken into consideration while traveling, regardless of whether you do so solo or with a group. By taking the right precautions, you ensure a good time that much more.

Part of staying safe and having a great time during your travels means being prepared, having a worst-case-scenario plan, and being ready for things to go wrong every now and then.

All that said, safety and being scared are almost never on the forefront of my mind when I'm traveling alone, even though friends, family, and media almost always bring up safety as the main reason why women shouldn't travel alone. I have found that I feel safer abroad than I did in my hometown, and that the precautions I would take there also make sense abroad, so I don't do all that much differently. Yes, safety is important, but it's not as big of a deal as you might think.

On The Road: *Tips and Tricks for Being Fearless*

Once you're on the road, how will you keep your budget in check, figure out where to eat and sleep, and how to get from point A to B? It might seem like a lot to think about right now, but things tend to fall into place and make a lot more sense once you're on the ground.

These are the best ways that I have found to navigate my way around the world on the ground, saving money, staying safe, and staying fearless.

Saving on the Road

The best way that I have found to keep my budget intact on the road is to do as the locals do.

What are the locals eating? How are the locals getting from point a to point B? How can I do more things the way that they would do it?

In the developing world, that will probably mean giving up some comforts. In the developed world, that will probably mean taking a bit more time and effort, such as cooking your own food instead of eating out at restaurants. Let's break it down by category:

Taking local transportation

In most of the world there are two options for getting from point A to point B: The tourist way and the local way. The locals have to get around somehow, and it's usually pretty easy to find out.

In Southeast Asia, that means taking the buses that don't have air conditioning. In Africa, that means taking the minibuses, which tend to be overcrowded. In Europe, that means taking the third-class train or a bicycle rental instead of a taxi.

If you want to go to the local route, go directly to the train or bus station and weigh your options rather than buying through a travel agent or middleman. (Always make sure that you keep a close eye on your bags when in train stations and transit hubs as they can be fertile ground for pickpockets.) If you run into a language barrier, write down the name of your destination on a piece of paper and show it to the person behind the counter and they should understand where you're trying to go.

The local method might take a little — or even a lot — longer and will probably be less comfortable. It will require more effort as well, since you'll need to get to the train station and buy the ticket, but it will be cheaper and it might give you some great stories too. I often prefer it for the last reason alone.

Tourist transportation will usually be available at your hotel or hostel and it will cost more. In most cases, it will also be more convenient. I usually do opt for the local method, but if I am in a hurry I might go for a taxi or a car rental for flexibility.

Accommodation

What's the best option for solo travelers in terms of accommodation? If you want to save money and be somewhere social, I would stay in a dorm. I usually pick by showing up to the destination and looking around, or by checking Hostelworld before I go and booking something with good reviews. Bring earplugs and a sleeping mask just in case.

I stayed in dorms for the first two years of my travels because I saved so much money and I loved the social atmosphere. These days, now that I'm a bit older and have a more robust budget, I still often stay in hostels, but I book a private room. That way I get my own space but I can also meet other people easily. It's still much cheaper than a hotel!

I also find that in beach destinations, I can usually get a basic beach bungalow for a small amount of money. In Mozambique, for example, I only paid between $15 and $20 per night for my own little hut with a fan. I still met plenty of other travelers by hanging out in the common area.

I also love Airbnb, particularly in North America and in Europe. It gives me a chance to stay in a local neighborhood, and if I rent a room in someone's home rather than the entire place, I often get to meet the local person as well. Sometimes I even hang out with them!

I am generally not a fan of hotels as a solo traveler. I find that the fancier they get, the more isolating they are as well. Plus, they blow your budget quickly. As I have gotten older, my tastes have changed as far as my traveling goes, but I still find that guesthouses in Asia, backpackers and campsites in Africa, and higher-end hostels in Europe are still a great fit for me and tend to accommodate people of all ages.

Food

Before traveling I never cared all that much about food. Sure, it's necessary for survival, but "foodies" confused me a bit with their enthusiasm. Then I came to realize that Sichuan numbing peppers are a unique part of that Chinese province's cuisine; fish sauces of varying mixtures and flavors are an important seasoning in Vietnamese food, morphing as one moves through the country; and the art of making sushi rice takes decades of practice and study to learn properly.

Food is a huge part of culture and an important part of the travel experience. Experiencing a place through its food offers some of the most authentic travel experiences possible, and it doesn't have to be expensive.

The cheapest and best food can usually be found by heading away from the tourist stretch. If staying in a beachy destination, that means going away from the shore, even just a street or two in, and finding a small local joint.

I generally have four rules for finding cheap and delicious food:

1. Avoid restaurant chains.

2. The menu should be in the local language (so learn the names of a few dishes before you go or take a glance at the meals other people are eating and say, "I want that!").

3. It should be crowded with locals.

4. Ideally it will be street food.

A word on street food: A common misconception is that street food is dangerous to eat or will be more likely to make you sick. This is typically untrue, particularly in Southeast Asia, where it's cooked right in front of you and was probably purchased from the market that same day. Go for the stalls that are crowded with locals.

It's also important to cook for yourself from time to time, especially if traveling through Africa, Oceania, Europe, South America, and North America. You'll find that most hostels and campsites have kitchens, and by going to grocery stores and buying raw ingredients, you can save a lot by making your own meals. Employ the same methods that you did at home when you were saving up: buy raw, cheap ingredients, at local markets when possible, and make meals that cost $10 and under. Offer to share ingredients with others when possible as well.

Finally, watch your party budget. Booze and bars will eat up your budget quickly, leaving you wondering how you managed to spend $100 in just one night. Limit nights out, or simply limit the number of drinks you order. I also find it's nice to opt for activities that aren't centered around partying, like hikes, free walking tours, and swimming at the beach. You can still be social without having to drink.

Budgeting and money concerns are a big part of the traveling experience, but with a good plan in place, and by spending wisely on the road, you can ensure that your budget goes a lot further. My top tip for saving is to pick countries that are cheap, where your money is worth 2–3x what it is at home. You can travel for so much longer that way!

Not Enough Cash? Work on the Road

If the part of the world that you want to see is expensive and you don't quite have the budget for it, there are ways to get there sooner. Many travelers take jobs while on the road in order to keep going or visit more expensive places. It's not as carefree, laidback, and selfish as traveling solely on savings is, and you may have to stay in one spot for longer, but if you want to keep traveling and don't have all the funds to do it, these are ways to make it happen.

Teach

Teaching English is a great way to earn money abroad and to have a high standard of living while doing so. In much of Asia, Europe, and South America, jobs are available for teachers with varying levels of qualifications.

Maddie, a former Tokyo-based English teacher I met on safari in Tanzania, saved up £10,000 ($15,000 back then) from one year of teaching English in Tokyo — one of the most expensive cities in the world — and used it to visit

Southeast Asia, Fiji, Australia, New Zealand, southern and eastern Africa, and the United States the following year.

When I lived in Taipei, Taiwan, my friend Robert had a system wherein he would work one year teaching English, then take one year off for traveling. The pay was good enough and the jobs plentiful enough that he never had an issue gaining employment again when he returned.

South Korea is another spot that is popular with English teachers, offering similarly high wages. Travel bloggers and former teachers Chris and Tawny Staudinger saved up for their travels by teaching in Seoul. Chris says,

We taught in a private academy. We made USD $2,000 per month, each, which is usual for a person with a bachelor's degree. We also got a signing bonus and our taxes and pension back (an additional $4,000) when we left. You should expect less as a public school teacher, or more in a university. The cost of living is extremely low, so you could comfortably save half of that a month, If you lived a Korean lifestyle and avoided Western bars and constant travel.

Keep in mind that the aforementioned countries have something in common: the jobs are reserved for native English speakers with university degrees. Experience is always a plus for the more desirable jobs with better hours and at more highly esteemed schools, which equates to higher pay but longer hours.

Teaching outside of school hours for extra cash is also a big earner. I earned $30 per hour meeting clients in Starbucks for private, one-on-one conversational lessons when I lived in Taiwan.

What if you aren't a native speaker of English? There are still options. When I stayed in Chengdu, China, I met Italian and French teachers who taught both English and their native languages to students who wanted to study abroad in those European countries. (The Chinese government is making a big push to bring in more English teachers and to increase fluency, so consider the mainland as an option if teaching intrigues you.)

As for resources, Matt Kepnes's step-by-step guide, *How to Teach English Overseas*, is helpful for getting through the process of finding a teaching job. *Reach to Teach Recruiting* and *Teach in Asia* are recruiting agencies for those looking to teach in Asia. And for a full listing of global resources, country-specific information, and TEFL courses, take a look at the *Go Overseas guide to TEFL courses*, which includes how to pick one and make sure it's accredited.

Work online

Do you have a skill that you can put to work while on the road? These days, as Wi-Fi becomes more prevalent and a greater number of people turn to the Internet to hire freelance contractors, opportunities for digital nomads are growing.

Plenty of people work on the road offering services such as website design, document translation, data entry, virtual assistant work, social media consulting, graphic design, interview transcribing, freelance writing, and a nearly endless list of other services.

It isn't easy, but with a good amount of diligence, self-motivation, and hard work, it is possible to build an entirely new career on the road. You just have to think about what you love doing that can be done remotely. Here's a listing of a few great places to look for jobs and to market your skills online:

- Upwork – various online freelance jobs

- Craigslist – any type of jobs

- People Per Hour – freelancing and design jobs

- We Work Remotely – various online freelance jobs

- Fiverr – design or marketing jobs done for $5. Not great pay but if what you provide is scalable, it could work out well.

- ProBlogger's job board for writers

- 99Designs for designers

- Power to Fly, a site that connects professional women

- Facebook groups for your industry if you're looking for virtual assistant work

Working online full-time while on the road is not without its difficulties. Perhaps you've heard the saying, "Work, play, or sleep. Pick two." Replace "play" with "travel" and the same is true of enjoying your trip while simultaneously trying to run a business. You're also limited to areas that have a strong Internet connection and have to accept that you'll spend a lot of time behind a computer screen when you'd much rather be out exploring.

Sometimes you'll have to pick between work and travel and as a freelancer; that means either missing out on a destination or a paycheck. The best way to enjoy both is to have months or years that are dedicated almost entirely to work and months or years that are more about travel.

Working holiday visas

While I was staying in Melbourne, I took up casual work at a high-end shoe store in a shopping mall to make ends meet. I couldn't believe how high the pay was — AUD $23 ($18 USD) per hour — simply for selling shoes. It helped to offset the high cost of living in Australia and also gave me an even better insight into the culture, interacting with tons of locals every shift I worked.

The jobs available to working holiday visa holders are often casual jobs like the retail job I had, or bartending and other restaurant jobs. However it could be possible to secure something in the field you studied and parlay that into a longer-term visa via sponsorship from your company.

Depending on where you hail from, working holiday visas present an opportunity to find work while living in a new culture and to develop your résumé. Many people leave dismal job prospects at home and reap the benefits of high minimum wages abroad, saving up and taking a year off in the name of travel thereafter.

Working holiday (or work and holiday) visas generally only last for one year. That time starts upon entering the country and does not stop if you leave. (Americans only get one year in Australia, while Canadians and Brits can potentially get two.) They are also sometimes limited to those who are 30 years of age and under, and most will require proof of sufficient funds for approval, which varies by country.

Hostel work

Mural I painted at Vientiane Backpackers in Laos in exchange for a free dorm bed, plus $100

If the thought of working online or in an office or retail shop or teaching in a classroom doesn't appeal, there are other ways to make a trip free — or much cheaper — by providing an exchange of services for room and board at hostels around the world.

If you like a particular location or hostel and have formed a friendship with the staff, inquire about the possibilities of staying for free in exchange for casual help where needed. This can mean bartending or working at the front desk, for instance. This is quite common in much of Southeast Asia and South Africa.

England-born Sherief, whom I met on Ko Rong, an island off the coast of Cambodia, is an example. In exchange for a bungalow that he shared with another employee plus free food, he staffed the bar most days of the week, working either a night or morning shift. The hours were long, and given how cheap the food and lodging is in Cambodia, it was not a great reward for his time. However, he would have been hanging out at the bar anyway, wanted to stay longer in Cambodia, and was running low on cash. To him it was a good deal.

Due to regulations on foreign work visas, most hostels around the world, such as those in Europe, South Africa, and the United States, can't hire foreigners as employees and therefore do not offer payment. Instead, in order to keep their business costs down, they allow volunteer arrangements such as Sherief's.

Seasonal work

Have you ever wanted to spend a season skiing in the mountains, guiding a rafting tour on a river, or teaching people how to surf in the sun? Lots of travelers earn their keep by working a season abroad as guides or instructors, and then taking the rest of the year off.

A great way to secure a job is to show up in person and network well before the season starts. It's possible to find a job mid-season in case other workers don't pan out, but don't count on it.

Cruise ships

The cruise industry needs literal boatloads of people with skills varying from customer service and food prep to guiding, cleaning, and performing. They tend to hire workers from all over the world, so it's also a chance to work with an international crew.

The hours and season can be quite long, but your costs are next to nothing while on board, so it's a great way to save up. If you have a specific cruise line or destination in mind, Google is a great place to start. If you're wide open and just want to see what's available, you can find listings on *allcruisejobs.com* and *cruisejobfinder.com*.

Crew on a boat or yacht

If you like the idea of sailing around the world but want to do so on a smaller scale than a cruise line, consider applying to be part of a crew on a smaller boat or yacht.

These jobs don't always pay and sometimes they require certain skills or experience, but many are looking for skills you might already have, such as cooking or cleaning. Such opportunities can be found on *crewseekers.net*.

Au pair

Do you love kids? Being an au pair is a great way to get immersed in another country and cut out most living costs.

While the weekly pay is usually more like a stipend, and you'll need to be available most of the time to take care of the kids, weekends and evenings are usually free. Plus, you often get to live in a pretty nice home! Find au pair jobs on *aupair.com* and *aupairworld.com*.

Become a dive instructor

I've met many travelers throughout the years who became dive masters or dive instructors so that they could stay in paradise. Popular places include the Caribbean, Southeast Asia, Central America, the Maldives, Mozambique, Zanzibar, and various islands in the South Pacific.

The pay is usually about enough to break even, so saving money is tough. You also need at least 50 dives under your belt before you can become a dive master, so there is some up-front cost involved, but it's a great way to get a job that's fun and keeps you on the beach.

To find a job, find a location and a dive school that you like, and see if they have any openings and/or a dive master program.

Volunteer

Working on organic farms, or *WWOOFing (World Wide Opportunities on Organic Farms)*, is a way to get accommodation and food costs covered in exchange for manual labor. It's an opportunity to learn about organic farming, with the added benefit of living on a beautiful farm. WWOOFing opportunities exist all over the world, and each is different. There is no standard length of time or set of expectations, so open communication with the host prior to agreeing to volunteer on the farm is essential.

Be My Travel Muse reader Katherine Wright says of her experience,

When I set out on my travels in 2013, I only expected to be in Europe for a few months. Then I started WWOOFing in Ireland at an organic farm. It opened up my eyes to the world of participating in a work exchange to enable long-term travel, while learning new skills along the way. Staying at each farm for 3–4 weeks allowed me to build friendships with locals and discover places off the beaten track. And since housing and food were provided by my hosts, I was able to save a ton of money.

I did something similar when I helped herd cows and built a basic website for a farm in South Africa. In return I had a chance to live with and bond with the family that owned the farm and to attend community events with them — a unique cultural experience I could not have had at a hotel.

At the same farm I met a family from Germany who found their way there through *Workaway*. They were helping to make mud bricks to build a structure on the farm that would eventually hold spiritual retreats. It was beneficial to the owners as they embarked on a new business venture, and beneficial to the family from Germany because, as a party of three, they were provided their own cottage, all meals, and a unique experience in South Africa that they could not have otherwise afforded.

Workaway opportunities come in a variety of forms, from helping out with gardening and livestock care in Bavaria, to digging at archaeological expeditions in Siberia, to translating text from Spanish to English for a yoga holiday company in the Dominican Republic, to name just a few. The opportunities are plentiful and available worldwide.

House-sit

House-sitting is an opportunity to stay in a home for free for a few weeks or even months. It usually involves taking care of pets or a garden while the owner is away. In most cases, there is no additional monetary compensation, though your host may ask you to pay for the utilities you use while in the home.

The competition to get a house-sitting job is stiff, and established sitters with positive reviews are more likely to get the opportunities. It takes a fair amount of time to apply for and search for house-sits, and each site has an annual membership fee, but for free accommodation, it can be worth it.

TrustedHousesitters comes with a $79 membership fee but is easy to navigate and has a large number of listings. A cheaper option is *Mind My House*, which only costs $22 per year but has fewer listings. For those targeting house-sits in Australia, *HouseCarers*, at $50 per year, is a good option.

Just as in the case with WWOOFing, it's important to have open communication with the homeowner to make sure that both parties are fully aware of expectations and limitations.

The above are the most traditional methods, but YouTubers, Etsy and eBay sellers, application developers, babysitters, importers and exporters, and all kinds of crafty and creative people have come up with ways to work on the road and make a traveling lifestyle a reality.

Working abroad is a great way to see the world and extend your holiday, begin a new chapter, or even find your new home. It's a bit more limiting than carefree traveling with savings, but it also provides another dimension to the travel experience. You get to interact with locals in a unique way, acquire a new skill, and maybe even learn a new language.

Think about what you're passionate about, and then think outside the box regarding ways to make it happen anywhere in the world. Whether it's learning how to bottle-feed sheep on a farm in Ireland, putting together window displays for a hobby shop in New Zealand, or even writing a travel blog, the options are numerous in our rapidly globalizing world.

How to Meet Others on Your Solo Journey

Most people fear that solo traveling means being alone all the time, but the great news is that you almost never have to actually be on your own! Travelers are friendly by nature, and chances are someone sitting alone would also like some company. If staying in hostels, you almost have to work hard not to meet other people, since they're such social places.

Even us shy types become very outgoing thanks to traveling. It helps us to relate to different people from all over the world, to learn new ways of thinking, and to better understand other cultures. Traveling solo has helped the outgoing version of me thrive and has boosted my self-confidence. It can do the same for you, too.

From the beginning of my trip, I found meeting others to be much easier than it had ever been at home. My first night abroad, I sat outside in the common area of my guesthouse on Khao San Road, smiled at a fellow female traveler, and before I knew it, I was sitting across from her at dinner. It was so easy!

The trend continued. I'd walk into a dorm room, insert myself into the conversation, and before I knew it, I had six new friends. It was sometimes as easy as walking up to a table in a crowded bar and asking to join. "Of course you can!" they'd always say.

I even made friends on long bus and train journeys. We had hours to kill, so there was plenty of time to get to know each other. I'd board a bus solo and emerge with a group of seven new friends. Really, it was that simple.

There were times when I wasn't feeling completely up to it, but I still went to the common room of my guesthouse or stepped out onto my patio in hopes of finding someone to talk to or hang out with.

I know I wouldn't have put even this much effort into meeting people if I hadn't been traveling solo. I simply wouldn't have felt the need to try that hard if I had always had a friend in tow.

Hanging out with the guesthouse owner's niece in Cameron Highlands, Malaysia

The following are great ways to meet all kinds of people from all walks of life on your travels:

Couchsurf

Couchsurfing is a community of travelers who interact in a number of ways, most famously by opening up their homes to complete strangers and letting them "surf" their couch for a few days. There's even an app now in addition to the Couchsurfing website.

Chantae Redden, a Southern Californian who has worked and traveled solo around the world, says of this method, "If I'm going somewhere that seems like it would be more fun with a friend to join, I put a travel notice and event on Couchsurfing that gives others a general idea of my plans. That way, other like-minded people can message me and come along."

I used it in Bangkok, a city with plenty of cheap dorms, because I wanted to have an authentic experience away from the typical backpacker digs. By picking a highly rated host and communicating expectations with him ahead of time, I ended up seeing a much more local side of the city, as he happily served as tour guide during his time off — and had a 37th floor apartment with an amazing view to boot.

If staying in homes of strangers doesn't appeal, Couchsurfing's get-togethers are a great way to meet locals just to hang out. That's how I met Francesco in Bologna, Italy. Though I already had accommodation sorted out, I wanted to have local interaction. I ended up getting a wonderful tour of the city by night on the back of his motorbike. I loved Bologna so much that I returned a year later, and that time I did stay with him and his lovely girlfriend, making tiramisu and eating dinner one night at the château (yes, château!) of one of his friends.

These daily, weekly, and monthly get-togethers of local groups are typically full of English-speaking locals and tourists alike and center around a theme, such as a street-food crawl event or practicing English at a local bar.

A word of caution: Unfortunately this community often gets criticized for becoming a way to meet others for casual sex. That's why it's important to communicate what your expectations are clearly with your host ahead of time. However, if things get weird, move to a hostel to get out of the situation.

Stay in hostels

Hostels are social places. Just about every country in the world has hostel options, with offerings varying from dorms to private accommodation.

Chantae adds, "While I usually like a quiet place to sleep, I make sure to choose hostels known to be really social every few days. Depending on what you're doing, it's usually easy to gather a small group of newly made friends together to join you."

Hostels often have organized group activities, common rooms and/or bars, and outdoor areas designed to promote a social atmosphere. Some even have organized meal nights, which are common in countries like China and South Africa and present the perfect opportunity to get to know others.

It's easiest to meet others in hostels or guesthouses geared toward the backpacking crowd. To find those with the highest ratings, try Hostelworld or Hostelbookers, which are owned by the same company but sometimes have different listings.

Look into organized events

Most destinations with tourist traffic tend to have organized events, such as pub crawls or day tours. Typically these types of events will be advertised at guesthouses and hostels in the area. You can look at flyers if there is a bulletin board at your hostel, or simply ask at the front desk when you check in.

If partying isn't your thing, look into tours that align with your travel style, and chances are you'll meet like-minded people. Do you love scuba diving? Look into a live-aboard boat tour, or if you're more the hiking type, check out organized treks or camping tours. Other solo travelers often partake in these experiences and are matched up in pairs by the organizers, to avoid the single-supplement fee.

I usually find these by Googling the destination name plus the type of activity I'm interested in, or by asking at my guesthouse or hotel.

Camping in a group of eight during a three-day trek of Mt. Rinjani in Indonesia, organized via my guesthouse

Both short- and long-term options are available all over the world. Not being a typical tour-taker, I was apprehensive about joining an overland camping safari for 35 days in southern Africa. My biggest fear was enduring such a stretch of time with perfect strangers with whom it might or might not be fun to spend time. I came away from it with a new appreciation for the occasional tour. I got to take a break from planning, had a wonderful time despite my initial fears, and made new friends in the process.

Download social apps

When it comes to meeting new people, Tinder may be the most popular application, but it certainly is not the only option available. There are now apps such as *Backpackr* and *Tourlina,* designed especially for travelers in the same destinations to meet each other, or even plan activities together.

Use Internet forums

In addition to Couchsurfing, Lonely Planet's *Thorn Tree forum* is another great resource, both for planning and for meeting travel buddies. Again, communicate far ahead of time before joining travel forces to make sure you've found a good match.

The *Digital Nomad Forum* is another excellent place to meet other travelers. Those on this board are a bit less likely to be low-budget backpackers and might be based in their various locations for longer. *InterNations* is helpful for new expats and is free up to a finite number of private messages per month.

Join groups

Reach out to your Facebook network. It's possible your friends already know people in the places you're traveling to. There are also plenty of Facebook groups out there that serve as great places to meet like-minded travel buddies; they are often regionally focused, like the *Southeast Asia Backpacking group* or the *Africa Backpacking group*. For something more female-specific, *Girls LOVE Travel* on Facebook is also a great resource for advice, meeting others, and sharing travel experiences.

In the case that you are a bit older, perhaps have a bigger budget, or simply want to get out of the backpacker mold, look at *A Small World*, which holds exclusive members-only events and is typically targeted more toward professionals who happen to be traveling, probably aren't staying at hostels, and wish to meet other like-minded individuals. The annual membership fee is $110.

Meetup is another worldwide option with dedicated interest groups of people who love things like food or hiking, or who share a similar profession.

How to meet locals

One of the most rewarding and intriguing parts of travel is meeting locals. Each place I go, the more I meet the more I learn about the country, my comfort levels grow, and my travel experience is enriched. It's worth putting in the effort to try to meet locals everywhere you visit.

The methods mentioned above are quite useful for that, including Couchsurfing, meetup groups, Facebook, and forums. *Airbnb* is also a good way to meet locals if you choose to rent a room in someone's home, or to participate in one of their locally led experiences. If you're a foodie, *EatWith* is a great way to meet locals and other travelers by booking a seat at the dinner table of a local.

In countries where most of the population might not be using or have access to the aforementioned methods, a good way to meet locals is to eat at the places where they meet. In some parts of the world, such as Southeast Asia or Africa, that means eating street food at night markets, or attending local events or festivals, which you can often find out about by word of mouth or by doing a quick Google search.

There has been more than one occasion when a local has seen me eating non-Western food and started a conversation with me out of curiosity. It's how I learned about the coconut festival in Nepal that I saw no other foreigners at, and how I've learned about other places to eat at or see that are off of the typical tourist trail.

Taking local rather than tourist-chartered forms of transportation, such as buses, trains, and boats, is also a good way to interact with a place's inhabitants. Even if you can't necessarily understand what's being said, it's a great way to become immersed in the local way of life and see what kinds of things people transport, how they dress, and how they interact with each other. If there is an English speaker on the bus, he or she is likely to approach and speak with you. It's an opportunity for him or her to practice English and for you to ask questions.

Heading off of the beaten path also promotes interaction quite a bit more than does sticking to the tourist hot spots. Being the only foreigner in a place, or one of just a few, drums up more curiosity. Also people in small towns around the world tend to be more hospitable and approachable than those in big cities.

The more you travel, the more your network grows as well. Tap into friend groups via Facebook and see if they live where you're going, might know someone who lives there, or can provide a suggestion, so that your chances of meeting locals are higher. Backpackers are a fun bunch, but it's nice to have to have a mix of cultural interaction as well.

Taking into account all of the above suggestions, the most important thing is to smile, keep a positive attitude and vibe, and remain open and curious. There's no telling who you'll meet, what new door may open, and what adventure could unfold.

The Gift of Solo Travel: *How to Take Full Advantage*

I'll never wonder what it would be like to sail across an ocean or move to Europe or just take a year off to chill out. I'll never doubt myself in a strange land, never be scared of languages or funky rooms... I won't be cynical about human nature, because strangers have helped me so many times.

My ripped suitcase, as it tumbles onto the carousel, is bursting with life.

—ELISABETH EAVES, Wanderlust: A Love Affair with Five Continents

I used to think that solo traveling was lonely, scary, and only for people who didn't have friends. Now I realize that it's the greatest gift that anyone, especially a woman, can give herself. It's a chance to see that there are other options out there than the traditional roles women tend to fill, and that life can be sweet with or without a romantic partner or friends tagging along.

Why Solo Travel Is the Best Kind of Travel

Solo traveling lets you follow every passion and whim on your journey. This is a chance in life that many people never get to have. It's a chance to be completely independent and to listen to yourself and nobody else.

Before I left, I asked the advice of my friend and Taiwan expat blogger Carrie Kellenberger, who said to me,

I traveled on my own for about a year and a half before I met John [her now-husband]. While it's intimidating to think about, I guarantee that it is going to change your life. In many ways, solo travel has made me completely fearless. I'm not afraid to try new things after having a go of things on my own for so long in Asia. You'll meet loads of single travelers, and I'm sure you won't have a shortage of people to meet up with.

She turned out to be completely right. There were tons of solo travelers out there —far more than I ever expected to come across. Some girls I met were only 18 and had set out to travel the world alone. It made me wonder why I had ever been so afraid of my own solo journey! In knowing that there are so many others out there seeking the same thing, it's clear that solo traveling doesn't have to be lonely.

It turns out that solo travel is getting more popular, too: 24% of people traveled alone on their most recent overseas leisure vacation, up from 15% in 2013, according to the 2015 Visa Global Travel Intentions Study.

We worry that as solo women we'll be targeted more, have more safety worries, and might find solo travel more difficult. I came to find in many ways that being a solo female was actually a big advantage. Locals took extra care to help me, as I was approachable and nonthreatening. I was a source of fascination since I was a woman traveling alone.

Solo travelers are also more aware of our surroundings. At a market, we're taking in all of the sights and smells with no distractions or reminders of home. Instead of worrying about a friend's good time, we're staring out the window and reflecting on the day's exchanges and experiences on the bus, enjoying the scenery, and listening to music. At a beach by ourselves, the entire vista is ours.

Swiss philosopher and television personality Alain de Botton said it best in *The Art of Travel* when he wrote,

It seemed an advantage to be traveling alone. Our responses to the world are crucially molded by the company we keep, for we temper our curiosity to fit in with the expectations of others... Being closely observed by a companion can also inhibit our observation of others; then, too, we may become caught up in adjusting ourselves to the companion's questions and remarks, or feel the need to make ourselves seem more normal than is good for our curiosity.

When Tough Times Hit: Combatting Loneliness

Dr. Seuss said it best in the classic *Oh, the Places You'll Go!*: "I'm sorry to say so but, sadly, it's true, that Bang-ups, and Hang-ups can happen to you."

There will absolutely be days that aren't amazingly wonderful, exploding with rainbows and sunshine, and they'll be that much tougher to deal with because you can't burden anyone else with your emotions, save for perfect strangers. You'll feel badly, because if this is supposed to be the trip of a lifetime, why isn't it amazing in this moment?

Just like back home in "the real world," there will be up days and there will be down days. The down days may feel more pronounced because just a day ago everything was so stimulating and beautiful, and suddenly it seems dark and lonely. Ashley Fleckenstein, former Paris-based au pair and travel blogger at *Ashley Abroad*, suggests the following:

To deal with down days on the road I'd highly recommend Skyping friends and family back home. When I was traveling for two months alone through Asia, sometimes I felt so exhausted meeting new people all the time, and I just needed to hear a familiar voice. I'd also recommend checking into a hotel or guesthouse where you can have your own space. There's nothing that cures a travel slump like a bubble bath and room service when you've been staying in crowded hostels for weeks.

In addition to her suggestions, try the following:

- **Forgive yourself** for feeling down or out of place. Bad days happen even on beautiful beaches and on the trip of a lifetime. It's OK, and it really does happen to everyone.

- **If you're lonely, move to a popular hostel**, even if only for a few days, in order to meet new people and feel the social vibe. This can be a massive help, as down days are often due to loneliness.

- **Leave**. If where you're staying is making you feel down, then move on to greener pastures. If you need to go somewhere familiar, see friends again, or change your route, that's OK, too. Solo travelers have that kind of freedom.

- **Stay off of Facebook**. The news feed full of memories of home and all of the things you don't have in the moment. It's not a helpful way of dealing with tough times and often makes them worse.

- **Use the down time** to read, do some reflection, and come up with healthy ways to deal with the difficulty of being alone on the road. Some books that have helped me through dark times are *What Makes You Not a Buddhist* and *The Art of Happiness in a Troubled World* (yes, written by Buddhist monks, but not religious texts), as well as the comic blog *Zen Pencils*.

- **Practice gratitude** for the good times that you've had. Remembering positive moments is a great way to get excited for the road ahead.

- **Try something new** — sign up for a cooking course, learn how to paint, sit with a blank book and sketch out your surroundings or write down your thoughts. Being creative can be very therapeutic.

- **Know that the bad moments will pass**, because nothing lasts forever, just like the good moments also unfortunately cannot last forever.

- **Remember that you're captain of the ship and the architect of your own happiness**, and by deciding to be positive and not following negative thought loops, you can make it out of the dark moments and find your way back to happiness again. By developing the ability to find happiness from within yourself rather than from the world outside and other people, your confidence grows.

The good news is that when the good days come again, they'll be beautiful, you'll meet more wonderful people, and you'll still be stimulated and enriched by all that you're learning, enjoying, and seeing.

Will Solo Travel Help You Find Yourself?

Ever since the book and subsequent movie *Eat, Pray, Love* came out, solo female travelers have either embraced or loathed the idea that they're out doing the exact same thing — taking an extended period of time out to "find themselves."

But traveling is, in essence, a voyage of self-discovery. If done right (read: more than just partying), solo travel should—and does—delve deep into the world within in ways most people don't expect when they embark on their journeys. Why? Nobody is influencing you anymore.

When on a solo trip you've worked toward and earned yourself, without the plans, budget constraints, or desires of anyone else encumbering you, you have complete freedom. When you open the door to the outside each morning, you and you alone get to decide whether you want to go swimming, hop on another train, turn right or left, meet a new person, go for a hike, or drink cocktails all darn day. You can make a plan, or you can pursue the day without any plan at all and see where it takes you. The choices are all, completely, totally yours.

I recall the first time it hit me how beneficial solo traveling is: I was in Chiang Mai, Thailand, a couple of months into my trip with Jahan, a friend I'd met at my hostel. We'd had a long day scootering around the mountains that surround the city, and by the time we got back, we were starving. When we ran into his group of friends, they insisted on eating together with us — but they weren't hungry yet; they'd had ice cream just an hour before. Frustrated, starving, and unwilling to wait for the group to get hungry again, I told Jahan I was going to do my own thing. I then had a wonderful solo dinner of street food, finished off with sweet mango sticky rice. I walked home that night with a full belly and no qualms at all about being on my own. I couldn't have done that in Jahan's shoes; he simply had to wait around, hungry, for his group to go eat dinner.

Chantelle Friesen, wedding photographer and part-time solo traveler agrees, adding,

I just feel I've grown so much as a woman [from my solo travels]. Fast-forward from ten years ago and I'm a completely different person! I'm more confident, more outgoing, and braver. I also don't care what people think anymore. I used to hate eating alone because I thought everyone was watching me, wondering why that loser was eating by herself, but now I can confidently walk into a restaurant and ask for a table for one and not be embarrassed.

Traveling solo, you are in charge of everything — the good stuff and the bad stuff. Choosing where to stay, where to eat, what to go see — that's the easy stuff. What about when your flight is canceled because of an erupting volcano, or you're lost in the middle of nowhere, or you have a toad the size of your fist in your hotel room? Being alone, you gotta step up and learn to deal with it all. There's no one there to do it for you.

[It] made me stronger. I dealt with everything that came my way. Now I'm not scared to go anywhere. The world is not as big and scary as I once thought.

Will you end up finding a version of yourself that you didn't know existed? It's possible that you will, but what's more likely is that the aspects of yourself that never got a chance to shine will come alive. You'll cultivate fearlessness, realize how capable you are, come out of your shell of shyness, learn how to talk to and interact with anyone of any personality type, and maybe even develop a new skill on the journey.

Moreover, as a solo traveler, especially female, locals tend to be intrigued by your story. They sometimes want to take care of you. It has resulted in a lot of adventures that I couldn't have had if I were part of a duo or trio. I'm more approachable as just me and able to say "yes" more often, when it feels right.

Solo traveling has made me grow despite the very occasional adversity. I don't sweat the small stuff anymore. I believe in my ability to do things. In a way, traveling solo has killed a lot of my fears and self-doubts.

When things went wrong, instead of stressing out and waiting for someone else to come up with a solution, I skipped the crying over spilled milk and got right to problem-solving. I didn't have a choice. *SOLO*

I actually have come to love and crave the challenge and the sense of accomplishment that comes with handling everything on my own. Things absolutely still go wrong, but now I'm prepared for them. Most solo female travelers echo these sentiments — and if it worked out so well for all of us, why not you, too?

Bon Voyage!

Phenomenal woman,
That's me.
Now you understand
Just why my head's not bowed.
I don't shout or jump about
Or have to talk real loud.
When you see me passing,
It ought to make you proud.
I say,
It's in the click of my heels,
The bend of my hair,
the palm of my hand,
The need for my care.
'Cause I'm a woman
Phenomenally.
Phenomenal woman,
That's me.

— Excerpt from "Phenomenal Woman" by MAYA ANGELOU,
American author, poet, dancer, actress, and singer

Throughout writing this book I often asked myself, "What makes male and female travel so different?" In practice it seems that there is little difference in the way that males and females choose plane tickets, board buses, meet other people, eat meals, and pack suitcases. The places we visit, the activities we engage in, and the local interactions we have on our travels are more or less the same, save for a few one-off stories or exceptional experiences.

In practice, male and female solo travel styles aren't so different. However if anyone had tried to tell me that before I started traveling on my own, I would never have believed it. Just as, before I discovered travel blogs, I figured that long-term traveling was reserved for the glamorous, the rich, or the extraordinarily brave vagabond types.

I never suspected that there would be so many women already out there traveling long-term by themselves. I had no idea that a girl like me, from a middle-class background, of mediocre bravery and with slim international experience, could ever survive traveling the world on her own.

Could someone who with so few real-world skills really hitchhike across China, trek for two weeks straight in Nepal, dive to 40 meters, learn how to say "hello" and "thank you" in over 30 languages, and see the world completely independently? It turned out that that brave girl was inside me all along. It was through solo traveling that I found her.

When I made the decision to go, it seemed like there was a mountain of obstacles in front of me, each one bigger than the last: I'd have to quit my job, somehow tell everyone about my plan, and endure it if I received negative pushback, not to mention the long period of slogging through the saving-up and organization phase.

However, each individual part of the process was doable on its own, and eventually all of those little pieces came together. By keeping my eye on the prize and not losing heart or sight of my goal, I finally took the steps and just went — and it was empowering to know that I had put myself there. When I left for my trip, I knew that I had earned it.

I came to realize the same was true of nearly every other girl I met out there who was also on her own. Each had gone to great lengths to make her travel dream a reality and became more resourceful, independent, and open as a result of her international experiences.

Solo traveling can fit any personality type. I met girly girls who stopped fearing spiders and shy awkward girls who slowly broke out of their shells, watching as those who used to spend hours at home in front of the mirror just let go and embraced their natural beauty. There is no special quality that only some people have that makes them a good candidate for traveling alone.

I hoped to demonstrate throughout this text, using my own experiences and the words of other solo female travelers, that it is not only attainable but even preferable to see the world by yourself, rather than traveling with a significant other, on a tour, or with friends.

Become confident in your abilities, know yourself and your own needs better, and learn how to interact with people from all over the world. Begin to see challenges as opportunities, trust your own instincts, and recognize your unique strengths.

Returning to the beginning sentiments of this book, in the words of explorer Amelia Earhart, "the fears are paper tigers," so crumple them up and push them down. The world can be yours — just buy that plane ticket already, and go!

— *Kristin*

Case Studies:
Solo Female Travel Inspiration

Women from around the world, of every creed and color, of varying ages and backgrounds, manage to travel solo. Here are the inspiring stories of several female solo travelers who have made the dream a reality, and the ways in which they did it.

Jaimee Ratliff

From: Memphis, USA
Age: 27
Professional background: Public relations

Jaimee took her first international solo trip to Europe for her 26th birthday. In the last two years her passport has accumulated stamps from Spain, France, Germany, Ireland, The Netherlands, Australia, Guatemala, Indonesia, and Mexico. She started traveling, because

[I] got tired of waiting for friends to be able to join. It's a frustrating thing when you have saved up the money and the vacation days, yet you feel held back because it's not the right time for others. I eventually got over my fears of

going alone and took the leap. It was the best thing I ever could have done. It opened up the doorways to really living life and increased my appetite for wanting to see the rest of the world.

As for dealing with naysayers, Jaimee says,

I believe people fear what they don't know, and unfortunately society and the media always portrays traveling abroad as dangerous. I typically respond with the fact that danger is relative and can be lurking right in [one's] own backyard. I also share my stories and experiences when I return from trips. When people hear of all the amazing people I met and see the vibrant photos in some of the most beautiful destinations, reactions all of sudden shift from "That's so dangerous!" to "Take me with you next time!"

These days Jaimee works in PR for a web design company. She also writes a travel blog, This Way North.

Dijana Stupar

From: Bosnia
Age: 34
Professional
background:
Registered dietician

Dijana is well into a year-and-a-half solo trip that has taken her through Europe, Australia, the United States, South Africa, Southeast Asia, and Central America. She started traveling after a breakup caused her to reevaluate her plans to buy a house. Instead, she took her savings of about $40,000 and traveled the world with it. She has no regrets, saying,

"I love me a lot more now — it is very nice to enjoy my own company and not always try to oversocialize with people. I have figured out that I want to travel more and learn more, and meditation has become very important to me."

Her top tip for saving up is to "stop drinking alcohol, stop shopping, and 'convert' everything to travel days to motivate yourself to spend less money while at home."

She maintains a personal blog documenting her journey at *Dive Move Sense*.

Wilaiwan Kanitjaratkul

From: BangkOk, Thailand
Age: 54
Professional background: Former engineer, now retired

Wilaiwan has been solo traveling since she retired from her job as an engineer in an oil refinery in Sriracha, Thailand, seven years ago. She has been to over 50 countries on her own. She travels solo because,

"if my friends go with me, mostly the trip is 10–15 people and they usually order too much food and wine. We all end up gaining weight. So it's cheaper as well for a solo trip."

She adds, "People in Thailand are not world travelers. Many times I got asked why I went to such countries...it is dangerous...it is dirty...[but] those countries are not bad at all. Good people are the majority and they are everywhere in the world. Therefore, if I like to see any places, I will just go. Seeing the world makes me a wiser and better person who understands different cultures [and] environments and respects their beliefs. After all I am just a short visitor."

Christine Amorose

From: Sacramento, USA
Age: 27
Professional background: Public relations

Christine has lived and worked all over the world over the past five years. She started out her career in high-tech public relations in Silicon Valley, California. She quit her job in 2010 to move to the French Riviera, where she started blogging, worked in a cooking school, and bartended on the beach. Then she moved to Australia, where she found a job in marketing and social media at a high-end furniture company. After testing the freelance waters while traveling full-time through Southeast Asia, she moved to New York City, where she now works full-time in brand partnerships at Vimeo.

For killing fear, Christine says

"I've always been pretty confident and thrived whenever people tell me that I 'couldn't' do something. When people were negative, I countered with the fact that I could get mugged or fall down the stairs or whatever awful thing just as easily in my hometown as I could abroad."

Read more at her blog, *C'est Christine.*

Tara Preissl

From: Vancouver, Canada
Age: 21
Professional background: Insurance brokerage

Tara shocked her friends and family by deciding not to go straight from high school to postsecondary education, especially given she was the "smart girl" in school. She had no real idea what she wanted to do but knew that she didn't want to spend the next four years of her life in a lecture hall. Instead she obtained temporary work. Of that she says,

I blame too many hours of being bored at reception for turning my dreams of traveling into a reality. I basically planned my entire first backpacking trip while sitting at various front desks in office towers scattered throughout Vancouver. After that first five-month solo backpacking trip, I went back to one of my temp jobs, where they hired me full time. I've been at this insurance brokerage for just over two years now.

She adds,

I remember telling two of my old coaches that I was going to be traveling solo. One immediately exclaimed "You're so brave!" And no more than a beat later, the second one said "Or stupid." I had mixed reactions, but I chose to first

surround myself with those that supported me, and then I learned that it didn't really matter what everyone else said, because this was something I knew in my heart I needed to do. People always think long-term travelers are running away from something — I'm not. I'm running toward something. Traveling makes me feel alive. Ideally I'd like to be able to find magic in my everyday life, but for the time being I'm happy to wander this world on my own. I'm excited to do the one thing that makes me feel alive.

Marilynn Smith

From: Nahcotta, USA
Age: 67
Professional
background: Artist

Marilynn started traveling solo after her husband of 45 years died. She found herself looking online at places to travel to, and finally one day she decided to just do it.

She says,

My husband and I traveled across the US in the late '60s; we camped everywhere. We raised a family but always took journeys together. In retirement we traveled and lived in Baja. I was not new to travel; I was just suddenly alone to do it all my way. I loved not having to compromise; it was now all my own new experience.

Her solo traveling ways have inspired her family members as well:

My lovely daughter is widowed and traveling this summer in a tent trailer with her two boys. They are visiting all the national parks she can fit in and having a ball. (She is a teacher and, after getting her second masters degree, finally has a summer for travel.) A single, widowed, working mom does not have a lot of money, but she does cook in, budgets carefully, hikes, sees wildlife and nature itself. Sometimes the best things in life are free. The only extra is her gas money. The gift is the memories she and her boys will always have.

Lauren Metzler

From: A small town in Oregon, USA
Age: 28
Professional background: Comic artist

Lauren started traveling when she was 16. She hitchhiked across the Pacific Northwest with nothing but a backpack and $50. She says of the experience,

I was a bit of a hopeless romantic, reading On the Road by Jack Kerouac and sleeping under the stars at night. After university, I was lost. I didn't know where to go, so I bought a one-way ticket to Southeast Asia five years ago and have been traveling ever since.

She has made her travels possible by working on the road, taking up jobs like teaching English, working as a barista, and even drawing concept sketches for a David Lynch short film. For those who are afraid of going against friends' and family's opinions by traveling alone, she says, "Remember, you have permission to be free."

Read more at her blog, *Love & Travel.*

Anne Davison

From: United Kingdom
Age: 59
Professional background: Civil Servant

Anne had a decent job, a nice home, a nice car and lots of friends & family but for as long as she can remember, she had felt a desire to leave everything behind and travel the world. Her wanderlust was revived after meeting and speaking with someone who had then been traveling for 14 months. She has since then sold her house, applied for a year of unpaid leave and left to see the world.

Her adventure saw her enjoying a summer in Ireland, participating a meditation retreat in the Pyrenees, traveling for a few months in Spain, Crete and Greece, celebrating her son's birthday in Barcelona, spending Christmas in Marrakech, and returning to Spain before spending a couple of months in Portugal.

For Anne, the reason for going solo is simple—no one was able to travel with her and she had spent too long waiting for the right time or companion so she just decided to go alone. Her advice to anyone who is in a similar situation is to

"Do it! Don't wait for anyone to do it for you, if you really want to travel then find a way and don't let anyone stop you."

Her plans for the future? She is heading home—to seek a second year of unpaid leave so that she can carry on traveling.

Denise Julieanne Collins

From: San Francisco, USA
Age: 48
Professional background: Attorney

Instead of sulking from a layoff, Denise took it as an opportunity and spent 5 months traveling in Australia and Asia in 2015. She followed advice from the book "*How to Travel the World on $50 a Day.*"

To stay safe—she always had a hotel booked for the first 2–3 nights in a new city, and she tried not to land at night. A woman operating on her own set of rules, she says,

"The one thing I disagree with is the advice to just bring a backpack. I brought a wheelie and a backpack and I am SO glad I did. A lot of advice I got was just to bring a few things—a swimsuit, sundress, pair of shorts, pair a jeans and a few tops. I was 46 and I wanted to look good! I brought 14 outfits and bought some clothes and jewelry along the way too. I had a full case of make up and skin care. I love that I am wearing different things in my photos. Bring stuff, ladies over 40!"

Maia Williamson

From: MOntreal, Canada
Age: 40
Professional background: ESL teacher

Maia first went to Europe in her early 20s with a group of girlfriends. She loved the experience and kept planning trips, and when people couldn't come with her, she went anyway.

"To be honest, I never planned to become a solo traveler; it just sort of happened that way, over and over again." She says.

She has been to over 40 countries and Africa and South America are her favorite continents. She has gone solo each time but met plenty of people on the road. The people she has encountered have always been so welcoming that she felt like she was leaving her family and friends even as she returned back to Canada.

"Why wait for someone else, the 'right' time, more money, a better plan? Tomorrow
isn't guaranteed to any of us, and if you don't go and see the world, that's on nobody but you."

Julie Crowley

From: Manchester, United Kingdom
Age: 57
Professional background: Personal and Professional Development Coach

Travel was a dream of Julie's for more than 30 years and when the stars aligned at last, she didn't dream of waiting for anyone else to join her, and went on a solo backpacking trip.

"It wasn't daunting, but exciting, to be going alone — doing my own thing, relying solely on me wasn't new, and the freedom to find myself again at a point in my life I was ready to change."

When it comes to dealing with naysayers, she smiles, quietly knowing for real that the world is a wonderful place, that it's safer out there than people may imagine and that, really, anyone can do it.

"You just have to want it enough like I did, I yearned to go 'one day'—I ached at the thought of missing out on

seeing with my own eyes what is 'out there', and that you will find a way somehow, someday."

Julie currently runs her own business, coaching for personal and professional development at Clear Mind. She also maintains a travel blog at Clear Mind Thinking.

Claudia Tavani

From: Sardinia, Italy
Age: 41
Professional
background: Lecturer
in
international human
rights law

After traveling to more than 10 countries solo, Claudia realizes that

"Solo travelers are actually hardly alone. Whenever I travel solo, I end up meeting way more people I'd actually meet if I was traveling with a friend, because I am way more open to new encounters. Solo travel hardly ever translates into being lonely. "

She pays no attention to naysayers, keeps a low profile to stay safe, stays in hostels and eats street food to keep traveling costs low.

Desi Pritchard

From: Oregon City, USA
Age: 54
Professional
background: Teacher

Desi decided to travel solo about 8 years ago.

"I was newly divorced and I wanted to see the world. I knew other women who were tied to their homes- their spouses did not want to travel, they could never find the money or they had commitments they felt they couldn't leave.

"I did not want to become one of those women who gave and gave to others, but not to myself. I also knew that there is an entire world out there waiting to be discovered. I felt that I had missed some of that when I was married- we had traveled a lot, but frankly, the compromising was difficult- I never wanted to look back and feel as if I had missed a huge part of my life. I was done with that."

To Desi, the decision to travel solo doesn't take bravery—it takes commitment. She trusts her own instincts and travel with a confident attitude to keep herself safe.

Besides her full-time teaching job, Desi opened a tutoring business and "every dime" from that goes towards travel and retirement.

Sophie Potvin

From: Canada
Age: 48
Professional
background: Secretary

For 10 years, Sophie planned a trip and every year she had to cancel for one reason or another. Newly single, she has no qualms about traveling alone.

"I plan my trips, I buy my plane tickets; if someone wants to join me, it's fine; if no one wants to join me, it's fine too."

After being tricked into an illegal teaching position in China, she was given the choice to either go back home or explore China—she chose the latter, and ended up traveling for 8 months.

Her advice to anyone who wants to travel alone is to

"take care of what scares you, make yourself feel comfortable. For instance, I'm always afraid of not having enough money and getting stuck in the middle of nowhere, so I put aside extra cash 'just in case', and I bring several bank cards and hide them in different places. So even if I lose a card or get robbed, I'll be fine.

I'm also afraid of getting attacked, so I don't go out at night in certain cities, and I don't drink. Whatever scares you, there's always something you can do about it."

Sophie is currently a full-time university student, obtaining her B.A. so that she can qualify for longer-term work visas, planning to graduate in 2018.

Ashley Yap

From: Malaysia
Age: 26
Professional
background: Digital
Marketing

Ashley packed her bags and boarded a flight to Surat Thani in Thailand after reading a blog post about a silent meditation retreat in Thailand. It was her very first time traveling abroad and alone.

"I never felt more alive. Every day was filled with lessons, surprises, new friendships and discoveries. Solo traveling and I were love at first sight and I knew right there and then that there was no turning back."

She then moved to and worked in Singapore to save up for a journey around Southeast Asia. When she reached her savings goal, she packed her bags and boarded another flight back to where it all started again— Thailand. She has since traveled to Cambodia, Vietnam, Myanmar, Laos, Philippines and Indonesia.

Ashley is a firm believer of the following quote:

*"And, when you want something, all the universe
conspires in helping you to achieve it."*
— Paulo Coelho, The Alchemist

3 months into her journey, Ashley told herself that she
wanted more, and,

*"Call it fate, coincidence or whatever you want, but the
next day after I told myself that, a job offer came up and I
now have the privilege to work remotely and continue
traveling."*

Ashley now works as the Brand Director of Be My Travel
Muse and she is planning to see Sri Lanka, Nepal and
the rest of the world next.

Wangechi Gitahi

From: Nairobi, Kenya
Age: 33
Professional
background: Marketer

A cancelled trip to the famous Maasai Mara National Park in Kenya with her friends left Wangechi feeling disappointed "at the prospect of not fulfilling a dream of mine and not so much that I wouldn't be hanging out with my friends." However she didn't want to miss out, so she went anyway and returned home with a new fire awakened. Her love of solo travel was born and has been growing since.

"I have grown physically, mentally and spiritually. It has taught me to be more independent, more self-reliant, more trusting of people and more open to the diversity in people. I have discovered willpower that I never knew I had before, I have learnt that its Ok to be afraid, to ask for help and to dare to make my dreams a reality. Last but not least I have made amazing lifelong friendships and grown in my faith."

Wangechi currently works full-time and runs her own travel blog to fund her next adventures.

Archana

From: Hyderabad, India
Age: 32
Professional background: Software Engineering

Born and raised in India, Archana moved to the States where she lived for 1/3 of her life before deciding to give up on the American dream and moved back to the Eastern Hemisphere to pursue a nomadic lifestyle.

"I have been known by my inner circle to be the kind of person who constantly strives
to break the stereotypes that are always trying
to define and confine me within the parameters of
being a woman, millennial, immigrant, and successful. I thoroughly enjoy fighting to take full control of what these parameters mean instead of letting the larger society define them for me. Giving up on a successful corporate career to embark on an indefinite backpacking journey has been quite instrumental in redefining my boundaries."

She adds,

"It's exhilarating to see that the world is so much safer, kinder and more comfortable than what it is made out to be. Making friends, the kinds of people that my previously definitive lifestyle would have never given me a chance to cross paths with, has been the highlight of

my journey. Confronting and challenging my own ideas of comforts, wants and needs and ultimately deciding what kind of lifestyle I would design for myself going forward and how much I need in order to really be happy, is the sort of learning that I have and still am enjoying thoroughly."

About Kristin

Kristin Addis is the author behind the popular solo female travel blog, Be My Travel Muse. For the past five years, she has traveled by herself all around the world, including spending a month or longer in every country in Southeast Asia, hitchhiking solo across two provinces in China, camping for a month straight in Southern Africa, and staying with a local family in the Maldives.

Her focus is on off the beaten path, authentic cultural travel all over the world. Once a former investment banker from California with very little international experience, she now bases herself out of her suitcase.

wandering world

Made in the USA
Las Vegas, NV
29 September 2023